Better Homes and Gardens.

ALL-TIME FAVORITE

Cake & Cookie

recipes

©1980 by Meredith Corporation, Des Moines, Iowa.
All Rights Reserved. Printed in the United States of America.
Large-Format Edition. First Printing, 1983.
Library of Congress Catalog Card Number: 79-93397
ISBN: 0-696-01215-4

On the cover: Fresh from the oven—*Marble Chiffon Cake* frosted with *Cream Cheese Icing* and garnished with orange slices, and an assortment of cookies: *Jam Thumbprints, Sandies, Pecan Pie Bars,* and *Oatmeal Chippers.* (See Index for recipe pages.)

BETTER HOMES AND GARDENS® BOOKS

Editor: Gerald M. Knox
Art Director: Ernest Shelton

Food and Nutrition Editor: Doris Eby
Senior Food Editor: Sharyl Heiken
Senior-Associate Food Editors: Sandra Granseth, Elizabeth Woolever
Associate Food Editors: Bonnie Lasater, Marcia Stanley, Joy Taylor, Pat Teberg, Diana Tryon
Recipe Development Editor: Marion Viall
Test Kitchen Director: Sharon Golbert
Test Kitchen Home Economists: Jean Brekke, Kay Cargill, Marilyn Cornelius, Maryellyn Krantz, Marge Steenson

Associate Art Directors: Neoma Alt West, Randall Yontz
Copy and Production Editors: David Kirchner, Lamont Olson, David A. Walsh
Assistant Art Director: Harijs Priekulis
Senior Graphic Designer: Faith Berven
Graphic Designers: Linda Ford, Sheryl Veenschoten, Tom Wegner

Editor in Chief: James A. Autry
Editorial Director: Neil Kuehnl
Group Administrative Editor: Duane Gregg
Executive Art Director: William J. Yates

All-Time Favorite Cake and Cookie Recipes

Editors: Diana Tryon, Elizabeth Woolever
Copy and Production Editor: David A. Walsh
Graphic Designer: Sheryl Veenschoten

Contents

Home~Baked Cakes & Cookies 4

Chocolate, White, & Yellow Cakes 6

Angel, Sponge, & Chiffon Cakes 24

Pound Cakes & Fruitcakes 34

Start with Cake Mix 40

Frostings & Fillings 48

Quick & Easy Cookies 56

Festive & Fancy Cookies 77

Start with Cookie Mix 90

Index 93

Home~Baked Cakes & Cookies

Cakes and cookies can make everyday meals special. Few of us can resist a freshly baked cake or a warm-from-the-oven batch of cookies. Rich layer cakes, elegant cake rolls, fancy cutout cookies, quick drop cookies, filled cupcakes, and easy cakes and cookies that start with mixes—all are in this collection of favorite old and new recipes. Accompanying the tempting recipes are special tips, techniques, and ideas to make preparation easier and add flair to your home baking.

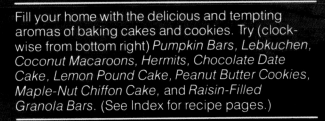

Fill your home with the delicious and tempting aromas of baking cakes and cookies. Try (clockwise from bottom right) *Pumpkin Bars, Lebkuchen, Coconut Macaroons, Hermits, Chocolate Date Cake, Lemon Pound Cake, Peanut Butter Cookies, Maple-Nut Chiffon Cake,* and *Raisin-Filled Granola Bars.* (See Index for recipe pages.)

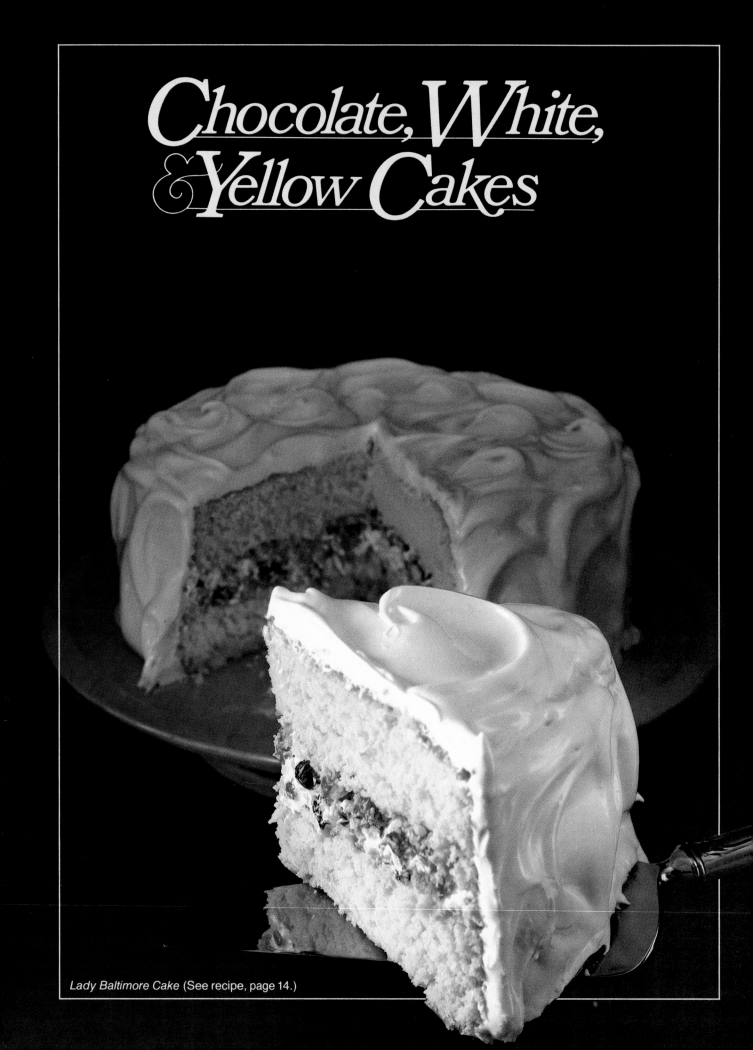

Chocolate, White, & Yellow Cakes

Lady Baltimore Cake (See recipe, page 14.)

Chocolate Cakes

Deep fudge, light cocoa, and German chocolate are just a few chocolate cake favorites you can choose from. Chocolate cakes have a light tender texture that results from creaming the shortening and sugar till fluffy, like other shortening cakes.

*W*hen preparing any shortening cake, grease and lightly flour the baking pans. Use folded paper toweling or a pastry brush to generously apply shortening to the bottoms and sides of pans. Add a little flour; tilt and tap the pan to distribute flour evenly. When the pan is completely flour-dusted, dump out the excess flour.

A shortening cake is done when a wooden pick inserted in the center comes out clean. To allow air to circulate freely in the oven during baking, be sure the cake pans don't touch each other or the sides of the oven.

*C*ool cake in pan on wire rack for 10 minutes. Remove cake from pan by placing a wire rack atop the cake and inverting the pan and rack together, as shown. Lift off the pan. Pans may be hard to remove if a cake is cooled in the pan more than 10 minutes. Because the top of a cake is rounded, the cake won't sit securely on the rack when inverted and could crack. To prevent this invert cake again on a second wire rack so the base rests on the rack. Cool thoroughly. Frost as desired.

*S*plit the layers of a plain cake and spread a filling or frosting between its halves to make it fancy. As a cutting guide, insert wooden picks halfway up the side of each cake layer, as shown. Use a sharp, long-bladed knife to slice through each layer.

Feathery Fudge Cake

2 cups all-purpose flour
1¼ teaspoons baking soda
½ teaspoon salt
⅔ cup butter *or* margarine
1¾ cups sugar
1 teaspoon vanilla
2 eggs
3 squares (3 ounces) unsweetened chocolate, melted and cooled
1¼ cups cold water

Grease and lightly flour two 9x1½-inch round baking pans; set aside. Stir together flour, baking soda, and salt. In mixer bowl beat butter or margarine on medium speed of electric mixer about 30 seconds. Add sugar and vanilla and beat till well combined. Add eggs, one at a time, beating on medium speed for 1 minute after each. Stir in cooled chocolate. Add dry ingredients and cold water alternately to beaten mixture, beating on low speed after each addition. Turn batter into prepared pans. Bake in 350° oven for 30 to 35 minutes or till cakes test done. Place on wire racks; cool 10 minutes. Remove from pans; cool on racks. Frost as desired. Serves 12.

Chocolate Sheet Cake (pictured on pages 18 and 19)

Frost with the chocolate frosting in recipe, or frost as desired —

2 cups all-purpose flour
2 cups sugar
1 teaspoon baking soda
½ teaspoon salt
1 cup butter *or* margarine
1 cup water
⅓ cup unsweetened cocoa powder
2 eggs
½ cup buttermilk *or* sour milk
1½ teaspoons vanilla
¼ cup butter *or* margarine
3 tablespoons unsweetened cocoa powder
3 tablespoons buttermilk *or* sour milk
2¼ cups sifted powdered sugar
½ teaspoon vanilla
¾ cup coarsely chopped pecans

Grease and lightly flour a 15x10x1-inch or a 13x9x2-inch baking pan; set aside. In large mixer bowl stir together flour, sugar, baking soda, and salt. In medium saucepan combine 1 cup butter or margarine, the water, and the ⅓ cup cocoa powder. Bring mixture just to boiling, stirring constantly. Remove from heat. Add cocoa mixture to dry ingredients; beat at low speed of electric mixer just till combined. Add eggs, ½ cup buttermilk, and 1½ teaspoons vanilla; beat 1 minute at low speed. (Batter will be thin.) Turn batter into prepared pan. Bake in 350° oven about 25 minutes for 15x10x1-inch baking pan or for 30 to 35 minutes for 13x9x2-inch baking pan, or till cake tests done.

Meanwhile, in saucepan combine the ¼ cup butter or margarine, 3 tablespoons cocoa powder, and 3 tablespoons buttermilk; bring to boil. Remove from heat. Add powdered sugar and ½ teaspoon vanilla; beat till smooth. Stir in pecans. Pour hot frosting over the warm cake, spreading evenly. Cool cake on wire rack. Makes 12 to 15 servings.

Chocolate-Cinnamon Sheet Cake: Prepare Chocolate Sheet Cake as above *except* stir 1 teaspoon *ground cinnamon* in with the dry ingredients.

German Chocolate Cake

1 4-ounce package German sweet chocolate
⅓ cup water
1⅔ cups all-purpose flour
1 teaspoon baking soda
½ teaspoon salt
½ cup butter *or* margarine
1 cup sugar
1 teaspoon vanilla
3 egg yolks
⅔ cup buttermilk *or* sour milk
3 stiff-beaten egg whites
Coconut Pecan Frosting (see recipe, page 51)

Grease and lightly flour two 8x1½-inch round baking pans; set aside. In saucepan heat chocolate and water till chocolate melts; cool. Stir together flour, baking soda, and salt. In mixer bowl beat butter or margarine on medium speed of electric mixer about 30 seconds. Add sugar and vanilla; beat till fluffy. Add egg yolks, one at a time, beating on medium speed for 1 minute after each.

Beat in chocolate mixture. Add dry ingredients and buttermilk alternately to beaten mixture, beating after each addition. Fold in egg whites. Turn batter into prepared pans. Bake in 350° oven for 30 to 35 minutes or till cakes test done. Place cakes on wire racks; cool for 10 minutes. Remove from pans; cool. Fill and frost top with Coconut Pecan Frosting. Makes 12 servings.

Cocoa Fudge Cake

2 cups all-purpose flour
½ cup unsweetened cocoa
   powder
1 teaspoon baking powder
½ teaspoon baking soda
¾ cup butter *or* margarine
1½ cups sugar
1½ teaspoons vanilla
3 egg yolks
1 cup ice-cold water
3 egg whites

Grease and lightly flour two 8x1½-inch or two 9x1½-inch round baking pans; set aside. Stir together flour, cocoa powder, baking powder, and baking soda. In mixer bowl beat butter or margarine on medium speed of electric mixer about 30 seconds. Add sugar and vanilla and beat till fluffy. Add egg yolks, one at a time, beating on medium speed for 1 minute after each. Add dry ingredients and water alternately to beaten mixture, beating on low speed after each addition till just combined. Wash beaters thoroughly.

In mixer bowl beat egg whites to stiff peaks; gently fold into batter. Turn batter into prepared pans. Bake in 350° oven for 25 to 30 minutes or till cakes test done. Cool 10 minutes on wire racks. Remove from pans; cool thoroughly on racks. Frost as desired. Makes 12 servings.

Chocolate Oatmeal Cake

1¼ cups boiling water
1 cup quick-cooking rolled oats
½ cup butter *or* margarine
1 4-ounce package German
   sweet chocolate,
   broken up
1½ cups all-purpose flour
1 cup sugar
1 cup packed brown sugar
1 teaspoon baking soda
½ teaspoon salt
3 eggs
1 cup packed brown sugar
6 tablespoons butter *or*
   margarine
¼ cup milk
2 cups flaked coconut

Grease and lightly flour a 13x9x2-inch baking pan; set aside. In medium mixing bowl pour boiling water over rolled oats; add the ½ cup butter or margarine and the chocolate. Let oatmeal mixture stand 20 minutes; stir till well combined. In large mixer bowl stir together flour, sugar, 1 cup brown sugar, baking soda, and salt. Add eggs and oatmeal mixture; beat at low speed of electric mixer till well combined. Turn batter into prepared pan.

Bake in 350° oven for 35 to 40 minutes or till cake tests done. While cake is baking, prepare coconut topping. Stir together 1 cup brown sugar and 6 tablespoons butter or margarine; beat till fluffy. Add milk; beat till well blended. Stir in coconut; spread over warm cake in pan. Broil 4 inches from heat about 4 minutes. Serve warm or cool. Makes 12 servings.

Baking Pan Variations

If you don't have the size pan specified in the recipe, use this chart to find an interchangeable size. Turn batter into greased and lightly floured pan(s). Bake in a 350° oven till the cake tests done. The timings given are baking guidelines. Baking times are based on 5 to 6 cups of batter.

Baking pan size	Baking time (350°)
Two 8x1½- or 9x1½-inch round baking pans:	25 to 35 minutes
Two 8x8x2-inch baking pans:	25 to 35 minutes
One 13x9x2-inch baking pan:	30 to 35 minutes
One 10-inch tube pan or 10-inch fluted tube pan:	50 to 60 minutes
Cupcakes (24 to 30):	20 to 30 minutes

Impress family and friends by serving this elegant *Devil's Food Cake* frosted
with *Seafoam Frosting* (see recipe, page 51) and garnished with chocolate curls.

Devil's Food Cake

2¼ cups all-purpose flour
½ cup unsweetened cocoa
    powder
1½ teaspoons baking soda
1 teaspoon salt
½ cup shortening
1 cup sugar
1 teaspoon vanilla
3 egg yolks
1⅓ cups cold water
3 egg whites
¾ cup sugar

Grease and lightly flour two 9x1½-inch round baking pans; set aside. Stir together flour, cocoa powder, baking soda, and salt. In mixer bowl beat shortening on medium speed of electric mixer about 30 seconds. Add 1 cup sugar and vanilla and beat till fluffy. Add egg yolks, one at a time, beating on medium speed for 1 minute after each.

Add dry ingredients and cold water alternately to beaten mixture, beating on low speed after each addition till just combined. Wash beaters thoroughly. In mixer bowl beat egg whites till soft peaks form; gradually add ¾ cup sugar, beating till stiff peaks form. Fold into batter; blend well. Turn batter into prepared pans; spread evenly. Bake in 350° oven for 30 to 35 minutes or till done. Place cakes on wire racks; cool for 10 minutes. Remove from pans; cool. Frost as desired. Makes 12 servings.

Black Forest Cake

    Cherry Filling
⅔ cup sugar
½ cup milk
3 squares (3 ounces)
    unsweetened chocolate,
    cut up
1 slightly beaten egg
1¾ cups all-purpose flour
1 teaspoon baking soda
½ teaspoon salt
½ cup shortening
1 cup sugar
1 teaspoon vanilla
2 eggs
1 cup milk
    Golden Butter Frosting

Prepare Cherry Filling. Grease and lightly flour two 9x1½-inch round baking pans. In saucepan combine ⅔ cup sugar, the ½ cup milk, chocolate, and 1 egg. Cook and stir till mixture just boils; cool. Stir together flour, baking soda, and salt. In mixer bowl beat shortening with electric mixer about 30 seconds. Add 1 cup sugar and vanilla; beat till fluffy. Add the 2 eggs, one at a time, beating 1 minute after each. Add dry ingredients and the 1 cup milk alternately to beaten mixture, beating after each addition. Stir in chocolate mixture. Turn into prepared pans. Bake in 350° oven for 25 to 30 minutes or till done. Cool 10 minutes on wire racks. Remove from pans; cool.

To assemble, place 1 cake layer on serving plate. Using *1 cup* of the Golden Butter Frosting, make a ½-inch-wide border (1 inch high) around the top of layer. Use ½ *cup* of the frosting to make a solid circle in center of cake, about 2½ inches in diameter and 1 inch high. Spread chilled Cherry Filling between border and circle. Place second cake layer on top. Frost top and sides with remaining Golden Butter Frosting. If desired, garnish with maraschino cherries and chocolate curls. Chill. Let stand at room temperature 20 minutes before serving. Makes 12 servings.

Cherry Filling: Drain one 16-ounce can pitted *dark sweet cherries*, reserving ½ cup syrup. Halve cherries and pour ⅓ cup *Kirsch or cherry liqueur* over; let stand 2 hours. In saucepan combine 4 teaspoons *cornstarch* and the reserved ½ cup cherry syrup; stir in cherry-Kirsch mixture. Cook and stir till bubbly. Cook and stir 2 minutes more. Cool; cover and chill.

Golden Butter Frosting: Beat 1 cup *butter or margarine* till fluffy. Beat in 2¼ cups sifted *powdered sugar* till smooth. Add 3 *egg yolks*, beating till mixture is fluffy. Add 2¼ cups sifted *powdered sugar*; beat till smooth.

Sour Cream Chocolate Cake

1¾ **cups all-purpose flour**
1 **teaspoon baking soda**
½ **cup shortening**
1½ **cups sugar**
½ **teaspoon vanilla**
2 **eggs**
3 **squares (3 ounces)
   unsweetened chocolate,
   melted and cooled**
½ **cup dairy sour cream**

Grease and lightly flour two 8x1½-inch or two 9x1½-inch round baking pans. Stir together flour, baking soda, and ½ teaspoon *salt*. In mixer bowl beat shortening about 30 seconds. Add sugar and vanilla and beat till well combined. Add eggs, one at a time, beating 1 minute after each. Stir in cooled chocolate and sour cream. Add dry ingredients and 1 cup *cold water* alternately to beaten mixture, beat after each addition. Turn into prepared pans. Bake in 350° oven for 30 to 35 minutes or till done. Cool 10 minutes on wire racks. Remove from pans; cool. Frost as desired. Serves 12.

Nut Cake

½ **cup all-purpose flour**
1 **teaspoon baking powder**
1 **teaspoon ground cinnamon
   Dash salt**
1 **cup butter *or* margarine**
1¼ **cups sugar**
6 **egg yolks**
1 **tablespoon finely shredded
   lemon peel**
1 **cup finely ground hazelnuts,
   almonds, walnuts, *or* pecans**
4 **squares (4 ounces)
   unsweetened chocolate,
   grated**
6 **egg whites
   Chocolate Glaze**

Grease and lightly flour a 6½-cup oven-proof ring mold; set aside. Stir together flour, baking powder, cinnamon, and salt. In mixer bowl beat butter or margarine on medium speed of electric mixer about 30 seconds. Add sugar and beat till fluffy. Beat in egg yolks and lemon peel. Add dry ingredients; beat well. Stir in nuts and chocolate.

Wash beaters thoroughly. In large mixer bowl beat egg whites till stiff peaks form. Fold about 1½ cups of the beaten egg whites into the cake batter; fold in remaining beaten egg whites. Turn batter into prepared mold. (Mold will be quite full.) Bake in 350° oven for 50 to 55 minutes or till cake tests done. Place cake on wire rack; cool for 10 minutes. Remove from mold; cool thoroughly on wire rack. Frost with Chocolate Glaze. Makes 12 servings.

Chocolate Glaze: In small saucepan combine ¼ cup *sugar*, 2 teaspoons *cornstarch*, and dash *salt*. Stir in ⅓ cup *water*; add ½ square (½ ounce) *unsweetened chocolate*, cut up. Cook and stir till chocolate is melted and mixture is thickened and bubbly. Cook and stir 2 minutes more. Remove from heat; stir in ½ teaspoon *vanilla*.

Peanut Butter-Filled Fudge Cupcakes

⅔ **cup packed brown sugar**
⅓ **cup milk**
2 **squares (2 ounces)
   unsweetened chocolate,
   cut up**
1⅓ **cups all-purpose flour**
1 **teaspoon baking soda**
⅓ **cup shortening**
⅔ **cup packed brown sugar**
1 **teaspoon vanilla**
2 **eggs**
½ **cup milk**
1 **3-ounce package cream cheese,
   softened**
⅓ **cup chunky peanut butter**
1 **tablespoon honey**
1 **tablespoon milk**

In saucepan combine ⅔ cup brown sugar, the ⅓ cup milk, and the chocolate. Stir over low heat till chocolate melts; cool. Stir together flour, soda, and ½ teaspoon *salt*. In mixer bowl beat shortening about 30 seconds. Add ⅔ cup brown sugar and vanilla; beat till fluffy. Add eggs, one at a time, beating 1 minute after each. Add dry ingredients and the ½ cup milk alternately to beaten mixture; beat after each addition. Stir in chocolate mixture.

In mixing bowl combine cream cheese, peanut butter, honey, and the 1 tablespoon milk; beat well. Fill paper bake cups in muffin pan ¼ full with cake batter (about 2 tablespoons each). Spoon about 1 teaspoon cream cheese mixture into the center of each; fill cups half full with remaining batter (about 1 tablespoon each). Bake in 375° oven about 20 minutes or till done. Cool on wire racks; frost as desired. Makes 24 cupcakes.

White,Yellow, and Spice Cakes

Among long-standing shortening cake favorites are white, yellow, and spice cakes. They can be as elegant as a four-layer torte or as simple as frosted cupcakes. The variety of flavors makes these cakes interesting snacks and special desserts.

*W*hen preparing a white cake, use only egg whites instead of the whole egg so the yolk doesn't dull the cake's whiteness. To achieve a light texture, beat the egg whites till stiff peaks form. To reach this stage, use an electric mixer or rotary beater to beat the egg whites about 1½ minutes or till the tips of the peaks stand straight when beaters are removed. Use a deep, straight-sided, small glass or metal bowl when beating. Do not use a plastic bowl because oils retained in the plastic prevent the whites from forming peaks.

*A*n important step in preparing shortening cakes is creaming the shortening, sugar, and vanilla. First, in a mixer bowl beat chilled shortening on medium speed of electric mixer about 30 seconds to soften the shortening. Then, add sugar and vanilla and beat, using a rubber spatula to guide the mixture toward the beaters. Beat on medium speed about 5 minutes or till well creamed, as shown. (A portable mixer may take longer.) Like chocolate cakes, any shortening cake batter should be poured into greased and lightly floured pans. A shortening cake is done when a wooden pick inserted in the center comes out clean.

Yellow Cake (recipe and variations pictured on pages 18 and 19)

2¾ cups all-purpose flour
2½ teaspoons baking powder
 1 teaspoon salt
 ½ cup butter *or* margarine
1¾ cups sugar
1½ teaspoons vanilla
 2 eggs
1¼ cups milk

Grease and lightly flour two 9x1½-inch or two 8x1½-inch round baking pans. Stir together flour, baking powder, and salt. In mixer bowl beat butter on medium speed of electric mixer about 30 seconds. Add sugar and vanilla; beat till well combined. Add eggs, one at a time, beating 1 minute after each. Add dry ingredients and milk alternately to beaten mixture, beating on low speed after each addition till just combined. Turn into prepared pans. Bake in 350° oven for 30 to 35 minutes or till cakes test done. Cool 10 minutes on wire racks. Remove from pans; cool. Frost as desired. Serves 12.

Individual Fluted Tube Cakes: Grease and lightly flour twelve 4-inch fluted tube pans; set aside. Prepare Yellow Cake. Turn batter into pans. Bake in 350° oven about 25 minutes or till cakes test done. Place cakes on wire racks; cool for 5 minutes. Remove from pans; cool thoroughly on racks. Makes 12 servings.

White Cake Supreme (Lady Baltimore variation pictured on page 6; chocolate chip variation on pages 18 and 19)

2 **cups all-purpose flour**
1 **tablespoon baking powder**
1 **teaspoon salt**
¾ **cup shortening**
1½ **cups sugar**
1½ **teaspoons vanilla**
1 **cup milk**
5 **egg whites**

Grease and lightly flour two 9x1½-inch round baking pans; set aside. Stir together flour, baking powder, and salt. In mixer bowl beat shortening on medium speed of electric mixer about 30 seconds. Add sugar and vanilla and beat till fluffy. Add dry ingredients and milk alternately to beaten mixture, beating on low speed after each addition till just combined. Wash beaters thoroughly. In small mixer bowl beat egg whites till stiff peaks form. Gently fold into flour mixture. Turn batter into prepared pans. Bake in 375° oven about 20 minutes or till cakes test done. Place cakes on wire racks; cool for 10 minutes. Remove from pans; cool thoroughly. Frost as desired. Makes 12 servings.

Chocolate Chip Cake: Prepare White Cake Supreme as above, *except* pour half of the batter into 2 prepared pans. Sprinkle a total of ⅔ cup *semisweet chocolate pieces* over batter in pans. Add remaining batter, spreading evenly; sprinkle with ⅔ cup more *semisweet chocolate pieces.* Bake as directed above.

Lady Baltimore Cake: Prepare and bake White Cake Supreme as above. Fill cake with Date-Nut Filling and frost with Seven-Minute Frosting (see recipe, page 51). For Date-Nut Filling, combine ¼ of the *Seven-Minute Frosting*, 1 cup chopped *pitted dates or figs*, ½ cup *raisins*, ½ cup chopped *candied cherries*, and ½ cup chopped *pecans*. Frost cake with remaining frosting.

Petits Fours: Grease and lightly flour a 13x9x2-inch baking pan. Prepare White Cake Supreme as above; turn into prepared pan. Bake in a 375° oven about 25 minutes or till done. Cool 10 minutes on wire rack. Remove from pan; cool thoroughly on rack. Cut into 1½-inch squares, diamonds, or circles. For icing, in a 2-quart saucepan stir together 3 cups *sugar*, 1½ cups hot *water*, and ¼ teaspoon *cream of tartar*. Cover and cook till boiling. Uncover; clip candy thermometer to saucepan. Cook till temperature of mixture is 226° on candy thermometer. Remove from heat. Cool at room temperature to 110°. Stir in 1 teaspoon *vanilla*. Stir in enough sifted *powdered sugar* (about 2½ cups) to make pourable consistency. Tint with food coloring, if desired. Spoon over cake pieces. Makes 36 to 40.

Busy-Day Cake

⅓ **cup shortening**
1½ **cups all-purpose flour**
¾ **cup sugar**
¾ **cup milk**
1 **egg**
2½ **teaspoons baking powder**
1½ **teaspoons vanilla**
½ **teaspoon salt**

Grease and lightly flour a 9x9x2-inch baking pan. In mixer bowl beat shortening on medium speed of electric mixer about 30 seconds. Add flour, sugar, milk, egg, baking powder, vanilla, and salt; beat with electric mixer till blended. Beat 2 minutes on medium speed. Turn batter into prepared pan. Bake in 375° oven for 25 to 30 minutes or till done. Cool on wire rack. Frost as desired. Makes 9 servings.

Guests will recall the old soda fountain favorite when you serve *Banana Split Cake* (see recipe, page 20) topped with colorful *Strawberry Sauce* (see recipe, page 53).

Silver White Layer Cake

2 cups all-purpose flour
1½ cups sugar
3 teaspoons baking powder
1 teaspoon salt
1 cup milk
½ cup shortening
2 teaspoons vanilla
4 egg whites

Grease and lightly flour two 8x1½-inch or two 9x1½-inch round baking pans; set aside. In mixer bowl stir together flour, sugar, baking powder, and salt. Add milk, shortening, and vanilla to the dry ingredients; beat on low speed of electric mixer till combined, then at medium speed for 2 minutes. Add unbeaten egg whites; beat at medium speed 2 minutes more, scraping sides of bowl frequently.

Turn batter into prepared pans; spread evenly. Bake in 350° oven for 25 to 30 minutes or till cakes test done. Place cakes on wire racks; cool for 10 minutes. Remove from pans; cool thoroughly on racks. Frost as desired. Makes 12 servings.

Buttermilk White Cake: Prepare Silver White Layer Cake as above, *except* substitute 1 cup *buttermilk* or *sour milk** for the 1 cup milk, reduce the baking powder to 2 teaspoons, and add ¼ teaspoon baking soda. Continue as directed.

Note: To make sour milk mix 1 tablespoon *lemon juice or vinegar* and enough *milk* to make 1 cup. Let stand 5 minutes.

Yellow Citrus Cake

2 cups all-purpose flour
2½ teaspoons baking powder
¾ teaspoon salt
⅔ cup shortening
1½ cups sugar
1 tablespoon finely shredded orange peel
1½ teaspoons finely shredded lemon peel
3 eggs
⅔ cup milk
2 tablespoons lemon juice
Lemon Filling (see recipe, page 53)
Fluffy White Frosting (see recipe, page 50)

Grease and lightly flour two 8x1½-inch or two 9x1½-inch round baking pans. Stir together flour, baking powder, and salt. In mixer bowl beat shortening on medium speed of electric mixer about 30 seconds. Add sugar and both peels; beat till well combined. Add eggs, one at a time, beating 1 minute after each. Add dry ingredients, milk, and lemon juice alternately to beaten mixture, beating on low speed after each addition till just combined.

Turn into prepared pans. Bake in 350° oven about 30 minutes or till done. Cool 10 minutes on wire racks. Remove from pans; cool. Halve layers horizontally, making 4 cake layers. Spread Lemon Filling between layers. Frost top and sides with Fluffy White Frosting. Makes 12 servings.

Milk and Honey Cake

1½ cups all-purpose flour
2½ teaspoons baking powder
½ teaspoon salt
⅓ cup shortening
⅓ cup sugar
1 teaspoon vanilla
1 egg
¼ cup honey
⅔ cup milk

Grease and lightly flour a 9x9x2-inch baking pan; set aside. Stir together flour, baking powder, and salt. In mixer bowl beat shortening on medium speed of electric mixer about 30 seconds. Add sugar and vanilla and beat till fluffy. Add egg and honey; beat on medium speed for 1 minute.

Add dry ingredients and milk alternately to beaten mixture, beating on low speed after each addition till just combined. Turn batter into prepared pan. Bake in 350° oven for 30 to 35 minutes or till cake tests done. Place cake on wire rack; cool thoroughly. Frost with desired frosting. Makes 9 servings.

Pineapple Upside-Down Cake (cranberry-pear variation pictured on pages 18 and 19)

2 TIMES
16 OZ
1 8¼-ounce can pineapple slices
2 tablespoons butter *or* margarine
½ cup packed brown sugar
4 maraschino cherries, halved
1½ cups all-purpose flour
2½ teaspoons baking powder
¼ teaspoon salt
⅓ cup shortening
¾ cup sugar
1½ teaspoons vanilla
1 egg

Drain pineapple, reserving liquid; halve slices. Melt butter in a 9x1½-inch round baking pan. Stir in brown sugar and *1 tablespoon* reserved pineapple liquid. Add *water* to remaining liquid to make ⅔ cup. Arrange pineapple and cherries in pan. Combine flour, baking powder, and salt. Beat shortening about 30 seconds. Add sugar and vanilla; beat till well combined. Add egg; beat 1 minute. Add dry ingredients and the ⅔ cup reserved liquid alternately to beaten mixture, beating after each addition. Spread in pan. Bake in 350° oven about 40 minutes. Cool 5 minutes on wire rack; invert onto plate. Serve warm. Makes 8 servings.

Cranberry-Pear Upside-Down Cake: In saucepan combine 1 cup *water* and 1 cup fresh *or* frozen *cranberries*. Simmer, uncovered, about 5 minutes or till berries begin to pop. Drain, reserving 1 tablespoon liquid. Melt 2 tablespoons butter or margarine in a 9x1½-inch round or an 8x8x2-inch baking pan. Stir in ½ cup packed *brown sugar* and the reserved cranberry liquid. Drain one 8½-ounce can *pear slices*, reserving ⅓ of syrup. Arrange pears and cranberries in pan. Prepare Pineapple Upside-Down Cake batter as directed, *except* use ⅓ cup *water* and ⅓ cup reserved *pear liquid* instead of the ⅔ cup pineapple liquid. Spread batter carefully over fruit mixture. Bake and serve same as Pineapple Upside-Down Cake. Makes 9 servings.

Peanut Butter and Jelly Cake (pictured on page 22)

2 cups all-purpose flour
1½ cups sugar
1 tablespoon baking powder
1 cup milk
½ cup peanut butter
¼ cup shortening
2 eggs
¾ cup currant jelly
1 package fluffy white frosting mix (for 2-layer cake)
½ cup chopped peanuts

Grease and lightly flour a 13x9x2-inch baking pan; set aside. In mixer bowl stir together flour, sugar, baking powder, and 1 teaspoon *salt*. Add milk, peanut butter, and shortening; beat 2 minutes on medium speed of electric mixer. Add eggs and beat mixture 2 minutes more.

Turn batter into prepared pan. Bake in 350° oven for 30 to 35 minutes or till cake tests done. Place cake on wire rack; cool thoroughly. Break up currant jelly with fork; spread evenly over cake. Prepare frosting mix according to package directions. Carefully spread frosting over jelly on cake; sprinkle with peanuts. Makes 12 servings.

Poppy Seed Cake (pictured on pages 18 and 19)

1½ cups all-purpose flour
1½ cups whole wheat flour
⅓ cup poppy seed
2½ teaspoons baking soda
½ teaspoon salt
¾ cup butter *or* margarine
1½ cups honey
1 teaspoon vanilla
4 eggs
1 small banana, mashed (⅓ cup)
½ cup buttermilk *or* sour milk
½ cup raisins

Grease and lightly flour a 10-inch fluted tube pan. Combine all-purpose flour, whole wheat flour, poppy seed, baking soda, and salt. Beat butter about 30 seconds. Add honey and vanilla; beat till fluffy. Add eggs, one at a time, beating 1 minute after each. Stir together banana and buttermilk. Add dry ingredients and buttermilk mixture alternately to beaten mixture, beating after each addition. Stir in raisins. Turn into prepared pan.

Bake in 350° oven for 50 to 55 minutes or till done. Cool 15 minutes on wire rack. Remove from pan; cool thoroughly on rack. Drizzle with Powdered Sugar Icing (see recipe, page 52), if desired. Makes 12 servings.

These homemade cake favorites are (clockwise from back left) split layers of *Yellow Cake* with *Fig Filling* and *Mocha Frosting, Chocolate Chip Cake* with *Lemon Filling* and *Chocolate Glaze, Cranberry-Pear Upside-Down Cake, Poppy Seed Cake, Individual Fluted Tube Cakes* topped with *Cherry Sauce, Chocolate Sheet Cake* with *Peanut Butter Frosting* drizzled with *Chocolate Icing,* and *Yellow Cake* cupcakes sprinkled with pecans and coconut. (See Index for recipe pages.)

Banana Split Cake   (pictured on page 15)

3 cups all-purpose flour
2 teaspoons baking powder
1 teaspoon salt
¼ teaspoon baking soda
1 cup butter *or* margarine
1½ cups sugar
1 teaspoon vanilla
4 eggs
1 medium banana, mashed (½ cup)
½ cup dairy sour cream
½ cup milk
½ cup instant cocoa mix
   Strawberry Sauce (see recipe, page 53)

Grease and lightly flour one 10-inch fluted tube pan; set aside. Stir together flour, baking powder, salt, and baking soda. In mixer bowl beat butter or margarine on medium speed of electric mixer about 30 seconds. Add sugar and vanilla and beat till fluffy. Add eggs, one at a time, beating 1 minute after each.

In small bowl stir together mashed banana, dairy sour cream, and milk. Add dry ingredients and banana mixture alternately to beaten mixture, beating on low speed after each addition till just combined. Into 1 cup of the cake batter, fold cocoa mix; stir gently till just mixed. Spoon the plain batter into prepared pan. Spoon cocoa batter on top in a ring; do not spread to edges.

Bake in 350° oven for 60 to 70 minutes or till cake tests done. Place cake on wire rack; cool for 10 minutes. Remove from pan; cool thoroughly on rack. Serve with Strawberry Sauce. Makes 12 servings.

Date Cake

1⅓ cups chopped pitted dates (8 ounces)
1 cup boiling water
1½ cups all-purpose flour
1 teaspoon baking soda
¼ teaspoon salt
½ cup shortening
1 cup sugar
1 teaspoon vanilla
2 eggs
¾ cup chopped walnuts

Grease and lightly flour a 13x9x2-inch baking pan. Stir together dates and boiling water; cool to room temperature. Stir together flour, baking soda, and salt. In mixer bowl beat shortening on medium speed of electric mixer about 30 seconds. Add sugar and vanilla and beat till fluffy.

Add eggs, one at a time, beating 1 minute after each. Add dry ingredients and cooled date-water mixture alternately to beaten mixture, beating on low speed after each addition till just combined. Stir in nuts. Turn batter into prepared pan; spread evenly. Bake in 350° oven for 30 to 35 minutes or till done. If desired, serve each piece with a dollop of whipped cream. Makes 12 servings.

Nutmeg Cake

2 cups all-purpose flour
2 teaspoons ground nutmeg
1 teaspoon baking powder
1 teaspoon baking soda
¼ teaspoon salt
¼ cup butter *or* margarine
¼ cup shortening
1½ cups sugar
½ teaspoon vanilla
3 eggs
1 cup buttermilk *or* sour milk

Grease and lightly flour a 13x9x2-inch baking pan; set aside. Stir together flour, ground nutmeg, baking powder, baking soda, and salt. In mixer bowl beat together butter or margarine and shortening on medium speed of electric mixer about 30 seconds. Add sugar and vanilla and beat till well combined. Add eggs, one at a time, beating on medium speed 1 minute after each.

Add dry ingredients and buttermilk or sour milk alternately to beaten mixture, beating on low speed after each addition. Turn batter into prepared pan. Bake in 350° oven about 30 minutes or till cake tests done. Place cake on wire rack; cool thoroughly. Frost with desired frosting. Makes 12 servings.

Gingerbread

1½ cups all-purpose flour
¾ teaspoon ground ginger
¾ teaspoon ground cinnamon
½ teaspoon baking powder
½ teaspoon baking soda
½ cup shortening
¼ cup packed brown sugar
1 egg
½ cup light molasses
½ cup boiling water

Grease and lightly flour a 9x1½-inch round baking pan; set aside. Stir together flour, ginger, cinnamon, baking powder, soda, and ½ teaspoon *salt*. In mixer bowl beat shortening with electric mixer about 30 seconds. Add brown sugar and beat till fluffy. Add egg and molasses; beat 1 minute. Add dry ingredients and water alternately to beaten mixture, beating on low speed after each addition till just combined. Turn into prepared pan. Bake in 350° oven for 30 to 35 minutes or till done. Cool 10 minutes on wire rack. Remove from pan; serve warm. Makes 8 servings.

Pumpkin Molasses Cake

2½ cups all-purpose flour
2 teaspoons finely shredded orange peel
1 teaspoon baking soda
½ teaspoon ground cinnamon
½ teaspoon ground ginger
½ cup butter *or* margarine
1½ cups packed brown sugar
2 eggs
¾ cup buttermilk *or* sour milk
½ cup canned pumpkin
¼ cup light molasses

Grease and lightly flour a 13x9x2-inch baking pan; set aside. Stir together flour, orange peel, soda, cinnamon, ginger, and ½ teaspoon *salt*. In mixer bowl beat butter on medium speed of electric mixer about 30 seconds. Add brown sugar and beat till well combined. Add eggs, one at a time, beating 1 minute after each. Stir together buttermilk or sour milk, pumpkin, and molasses. Add dry ingredients and buttermilk mixture alternately to beaten mixture, beating on low speed after each addition till just combined. Turn into prepared pan. Bake in 350° oven for 30 to 35 minutes or till done. Cool on wire rack. Sprinkle with powdered sugar, if desired. Serves 12.

Carrot Cake

2 cups all-purpose flour
2 cups sugar
1 teaspoon baking powder
1 teaspoon baking soda
1 teaspoon salt
1 teaspoon ground cinnamon
3 cups finely shredded carrot
1 cup cooking oil
4 eggs
Cream Cheese Frosting (see recipe, page 51)

Grease and lightly flour a 13x9x2-inch baking pan or two 9x1½-inch round baking pans. In mixer bowl stir together flour, sugar, baking powder, soda, salt, and cinnamon. Add shredded carrot, oil, and eggs; beat with electric mixer till well combined. Beat on medium speed for 2 minutes. Turn into prepared pan(s). Bake in 325° oven for 50 to 60 minutes in the 13x9x2-inch pan or till cake tests done. (For two 9-inch layers, bake in 325° oven about 40 minutes or till cakes test done.) Cool on wire rack. (Remove layers from pans after cooling 10 minutes. Cool well.) Frost with Cream Cheese Frosting. Makes 12 servings.

Cake Making Tips

For best cake baking results, leave the eggs, milk, and butter, margarine, or shortening to be used in the cake at room temperature about 1 hour before preparing the batter. This will improve the volume of your cake.

While beating the batter with an electric mixer, don't leave cake. Stay nearby, occasionally scraping sides with a rubber scraper so the batter will be evenly mixed and free of lumps.

Try something new for dessert. *Peanut Butter and Jelly Cake* (see recipe, page 17) and spicy *Dutch Apple Cake* are guaranteed to draw applause.

Dutch Apple Cake

2 cups all-purpose flour
1 teaspoon baking soda
1 teaspoon salt
1 teaspoon ground cinnamon
4 medium cooking apples
2 eggs
1 teaspoon vanilla
1 cup cooking oil
1½ cups sugar
1 cup finely chopped walnuts
Powdered Sugar Icing (see recipe, page 52)

Grease and lightly flour a 9-inch tube pan. Stir together flour, baking soda, salt, and cinnamon. Peel, core, and finely chop apples; set aside. In large mixer bowl stir together eggs and vanilla; beat on high speed of electric mixer for 2 minutes or till light. Gradually add oil, beating for 2 minutes or till thick. Gradually beat in sugar. Add dry ingredients, apples, and walnuts alternately to beaten mixture, beating well after each addition. Beat at medium speed for 3 minutes. Turn batter into prepared pan. Bake in 350° oven for 55 to 60 minutes or till cake tests done. Place cake on wire rack; cool for 10 to 15 minutes. Remove from pan; cool thoroughly on rack. Drizzle with Powdered Sugar Icing. Makes 12 servings.

Buttery Cinnamon Cake

2 cups all-purpose flour
1 tablespoon baking powder
1 teaspoon ground cinnamon
¾ teaspoon salt
⅔ cup shortening
1⅓ cups sugar
1½ teaspoons vanilla
3 eggs
⅔ cup milk
½ cup sugar
6 tablespoons butter *or* margarine
⅓ cup water
1 teaspoon vanilla
¾ teaspoon ground cinnamon
Sifted powdered sugar (optional)

Grease and lightly flour a 10-inch fluted tube pan or a 10-inch tube pan. Stir together flour, baking powder, 1 teaspoon cinnamon, and salt. Beat shortening about 30 seconds. Add 1⅓ cups sugar and 1½ teaspoons vanilla and beat till fluffy. Add eggs, one at a time, beating 1 minute after each. Add dry ingredients and milk alternately to beaten mixture, beating after each addition. Turn into pan. Bake in 350° oven about 40 minutes or till done. Cool 5 minutes on wire rack.

Meanwhile for cinnamon syrup, in saucepan combine ½ cup sugar, butter, water, 1 teaspoon vanilla, and ¾ teaspoon cinnamon. Heat and stir till butter melts; do not boil. Remove cake from pan; place on wire rack. Prick with long-tined fork. Place wire rack over tray to catch syrup. Spoon hot syrup over hot cake. Respoon excess syrup. Cool. Sprinkle with sifted powdered sugar, if desired. Makes 12 servings.

High Altitude Baking Chart

Cakes baked in a high altitude area (3,000 feet or more above sea level) usually turn out poorly. To improve cakes use this chart as a cake baking guide to adjust all ingredients listed. Experiment with each recipe to discover the best formula; where two amounts appear, try the smaller first and adjust next time, if necessary.

Cookies are more stable than cakes and need little adjustment. Experiment, reducing sugar and baking powder and increasing liquid.

Ingredients	3,000 feet	5,000 feet	7,000 feet
Liquid: Add for each cup	1 to 2 tablespoons	2 to 4 tablespoons	3 to 4 tablespoons
Baking powder: Decrease for each teaspoon	⅛ teaspoon	⅛ teaspoon to ¼ teaspoon	¼ teaspoon
Sugar: Decrease for each cup	0 to 1 tablespoon	0 to 2 tablespoons	1 to 3 tablespoons

Angel, Sponge, & Chiffon Cakes

Almond Raspberry
Torte (See recipe, page 27.)

Angel and Sponge Cakes

Angel and sponge cakes get their light, delicate texture from air in the batter. Beating egg whites and yolks properly, folding in lightly, and having an accurate oven temperature help incorporate and keep air in the batter.

*T*o make a sponge cake, place egg yolks in a small mixer bowl. Beat at high speed of electric mixer about 6 minutes or till thickened and a light, creamy yellow (lemon-colored). When yolks are sufficiently beaten, they will flow in a thick stream from the lifted beaters, as shown.

*T*o make an angel or sponge cake, place egg whites and cream of tartar in a large mixer bowl. Wash beaters well after beating yolks. Beat with electric mixer till soft peaks form. Gradually add sugar, about 2 tablespoons at a time, beating at high speed till stiff peaks form and stand straight when beaters are removed.

*G*ently blend ingredients into beaten egg whites using a folding motion. To fold, cut down through the mixture with a rubber spatula; scrape across bottom of bowl and bring spatula up and over mixture, close to the surface. Repeat this circular down-up-and-over motion just till blended, turning the bowl as you work.

*F*or a high tube cake, turn batter into an *ungreased* 10-inch tube pan. With narrow spatula, cut through batter to remove air bubbles. Place on the rack in the center of the oven. Bake until cake springs back and leaves no imprint when lightly touched. It will shrink slightly from sides of pan.

*I*nvert cake (still in pan) and place on counter to cool thoroughly. Inverting the pan prevents the cake from losing volume while cooling. If the cake pan doesn't have long enough legs, invert the pan and set the tube over a narrow-neck bottle to cool.

*T*o remove cake, set pan right side up. With a narrow spatula, loosen cake from edges of pan and center tube. Hold onto center tube and carefully lift out removable bottom. To loosen cake, slide a narrow spatula between cake and bottom. Invert cake onto a plate, letting it slip out of the tube.

Angel Cake

1½ **cups sifted powdered sugar**
1 **cup sifted cake flour *or sifted***
   all-purpose flour
1½ **cups egg whites (11 or 12 large)**
1½ **teaspoons cream of tartar**
1 **teaspoon vanilla**
¼ **teaspoon salt**
1 **cup sugar**

Sift together powdered sugar and cake or all-purpose flour; repeat sifting twice. In a large mixer bowl beat egg whites, cream of tartar, vanilla, and salt at medium speed of electric mixer till soft peaks form. Gradually add sugar, about 2 tablespoons at a time. Continue beating at high speed till stiff peaks form. Sift about ¼ of the flour mixture over egg whites; fold in lightly by hand. If bowl is too small, transfer to a larger bowl. Repeat with remaining flour mixture, ¼ at a time. Turn into an *ungreased* 10-inch tube pan.* Bake on lowest rack in a 350° oven about 40 minutes or till cake tests done. Invert cake in pan; cool thoroughly. Remove from pan. Serves 12.

*Note: Or, for angel cake loaves turn batter into 2 *ungreased* 9x5x3-inch loaf pans. Bake in a 350° oven about 25 minutes. Invert in pans; rest edges on canned goods. Cool.

Strawberry Angel Cake: Prepare Angel Cake as above; cool and remove from pan. In saucepan combine one 3-ounce package *strawberry-flavored gelatin* and ½ cup *water*. Heat and stir till gelatin is dissolved. Remove from heat. Stir in one 10-ounce package frozen sliced *strawberries*. Chill till the consistency of unbeaten egg whites (partially set). Beat ½ cup *whipping cream* till soft peaks form; fold into gelatin mixture. Chill till it mounds when spooned.

Cut cake horizontally into 3 layers. Spread gelatin mixture between layers; chill till firm. Just before serving, beat ½ cup *whipping cream* and 1 tablespoon *sugar* till stiff peaks form. Spread over top of cake.

Chocolate Angel Loaf

⅓ **cup sifted cake flour *or***
   all-purpose flour
¼ **cup sugar**
3 **tablespoons unsweetened**
   cocoa powder
6 **egg whites**
1 **teaspoon vanilla**
½ **teaspoon cream of tartar**
   Dash salt
½ **cup sugar**
   Vanilla Cream Filling (see
   recipe, page 52)
   Powdered sugar

Sift together cake or all-purpose flour, ¼ cup sugar, and cocoa powder; repeat sifting. In a large mixer bowl beat egg whites, vanilla, cream of tartar, and salt with electric mixer till soft peaks form. Gradually add ½ cup sugar; continue beating till stiff peaks form. Sift about ⅓ of the flour-cocoa mixture over egg whites; fold in lightly by hand. Repeat with remaining flour-cocoa mixture, ⅓ at a time. Turn into an *ungreased* 9x5x3-inch loaf pan. Bake in a 375° oven about 25 minutes or till done. Invert cake in pan, resting edges of pan on canned goods; cool thoroughly. Loosen cake; remove from pan. Cut cake horizontally into 3 layers. Spread Vanilla Cream Filling between layers. Sift powdered sugar over top of cake. Makes 8 servings.

Easy Angel Dessert

1 **cup sifted powdered sugar**
1 **3-ounce package cream cheese,**
   softened
1 **1½-ounce envelope dessert**
   topping mix
5 **cups angel cake cubes**
1 **21-ounce can cherry, blueberry,**
   ***or* strawberry pie filling**

In a large mixer bowl gradually add powdered sugar to cream cheese, beating till fluffy. Prepare topping mix according to package directions; fold into cream cheese mixture. Fold in angel cake cubes. Turn into an 11x7x1½-inch pan or a 12x7½x2-inch dish. Spread pie filling over top. Cover and chill several hours or overnight. Makes 9 servings.

Sponge Cake

6 **egg yolks**
½ **cup cold water**
1 **teaspoon finely shredded**
   lemon peel
1 **teaspoon vanilla**
½ **cup sugar**
1¼ **cups all-purpose flour**
⅓ **cup sugar**
¼ **teaspoon salt**
6 **egg whites**
1 **teaspoon cream of tartar**
½ **cup sugar**

In a small mixer bowl beat yolks at high speed of electric mixer 6 minutes or till thick and lemon-colored. Add water, lemon peel, and vanilla. Gradually add ½ cup sugar, beating till sugar dissolves. Combine flour, ⅓ cup sugar, and salt. Gradually add about ¼ flour mixture to yolk mixture, beating at low speed till blended. Repeat with remaining flour mixture, ¼ at a time, beating a total of 2 minutes.

Thoroughly wash beaters. In a large mixer bowl beat egg whites and cream of tartar till soft peaks form. Gradually add ½ cup sugar, beating till stiff peaks form. Stir about *1 cup* of the egg whites into yolk mixture. By hand, fold yolk mixture into remaining egg whites. Turn into an *ungreased* 10-inch tube pan. Bake in a 325° oven for 55 to 60 minutes or till cake tests done. Invert cake in pan; cool thoroughly. Loosen; remove from pan. Makes 12 servings.

Boston Cream Pie

The cake in this recipe is a Hot Milk Sponge Cake. If you like, bake the batter in a greased 9x9x2-inch baking pan as directed. Frost with a favorite frosting —

2 **eggs**
1 **cup sugar**
1 **cup all-purpose flour**
1 **teaspoon baking powder**
½ **cup milk**
2 **tablespoons butter**
   Vanilla Cream Filling (see
      recipe, page 52)
   Chocolate Glaze (see
      recipe, page 12)

Grease and flour a 9x1½-inch round baking pan. In a small mixer bowl beat whole eggs at high speed of electric mixer 4 minutes or till thick and lemon-colored. Gradually add sugar, beating at medium speed 4 to 5 minutes or till sugar is nearly dissolved. Mix flour, baking powder, and ¼ teaspoon *salt*. Add to egg mixture; stir just till blended.

In small saucepan heat milk and butter till butter melts; stir into batter. Beat at low speed till well mixed. Turn into pan. Bake in a 350° oven for 25 to 30 minutes or till done. Cool 10 minutes on wire rack. Remove from pan; cool thoroughly. Split cake horizontally into 2 layers. Fill with Vanilla Cream Filling. Spread Chocolate Glaze over top of cake, drizzling down sides. Makes 8 servings.

Almond Raspberry Torte (pictured on page 24)

8 **egg yolks**
1 **teaspoon finely shredded**
   lemon peel
1 **teaspoon vanilla**
1¼ **cups sugar**
¾ **cup milk**
6 **tablespoons butter** *or*
   margarine
1¼ **cups all-purpose flour**
1½ **teaspoons baking powder**
¾ **teaspoon salt**
   Almond Filling
½ **cup seedless red raspberry**
   preserves
½ **cup whipping cream**

Grease and flour two 8x1½-inch round baking pans. Beat egg yolks about 6 minutes or till thick and lemon-colored. Add lemon peel and vanilla. Gradually beat in sugar. Heat milk and butter till butter melts. Gradually stir about *half* the milk mixture into yolk mixture. Combine flour, baking powder, and salt. By hand, fold flour mixture into egg mixture. Stir in remaining milk mixture. Turn into pans. Bake in a 350° oven about 30 minutes or till done. Cool 10 minutes on wire racks. Remove from pans; cool.

Cut layers in half horizontally. To assemble, spread 1 cake slice with ⅓ of the Almond Filling, then with about 2 tablespoons preserves. Repeat layers 2 more times. Top with final slice. Spread with remaining preserves. Whip cream to stiff peaks; pipe or spread over top. Serves 12.

Almond Filling: In small mixer bowl crumble one 8-ounce can *almond paste*. Beat in 6 tablespoons softened *butter*. Add 2 tablespoons *light rum*; beat till smooth.

Chiffon Cakes

Combining the characteristics of angel, sponge, and shortening cakes, chiffon cakes are light and rich. These delicate cakes are made with cooking oil instead of solid shortening and use stiffly beaten egg whites to help in leavening.

*I*n a large mixer bowl sift together dry ingredients; make a well in the center. Add cooking oil, egg yolks, liquids, and flavorings, in that order. Beat at low speed of electric mixer till combined, then at high speed about 5 minutes or till satin smooth. When the mixture is sufficiently beaten, it will flow in a thick stream from the lifted beaters, as shown.

*T*horoughly wash beaters. (If any egg yolk or oil mixes into the egg whites, they will not expand to their proper volume.) In a large mixing bowl beat egg whites and cream of tartar till stiff peaks form and stand straight when beaters are removed. Pour the egg yolk mixture in a thin steady stream over the entire surface of the stiffly beaten egg whites.

*G*ently fold yolk mixture into egg whites. To fold, cut down through mixture with a rubber spatula; scrape across bottom and bring spatula up and over mixture, close to surface. Repeat this circular down-up-and-over motion, turning bowl as you work. Do not stir; this breaks down the air-retaining structure and fluffy consistency of the beaten whites.

Bake cake as directed. To test doneness, see page 25.

Maple-Nut Chiffon Cake (pictured on pages 4 and 5)

2¼ cups sifted cake flour *or* 2 cups all-purpose flour
¾ cup sugar
1 tablespoon baking powder
1 teaspoon salt
¾ cup packed brown sugar
½ cup cooking oil
5 egg yolks
¾ cup cold water
2 teaspoons maple flavoring
1 cup finely chopped walnuts
8 egg whites
½ teaspoon cream of tartar
Sweetened whipped cream

In a large mixer bowl sift together cake or all-purpose flour, sugar, baking powder, and salt; stir in brown sugar. Make a well in the center. Add cooking oil, egg yolks, water, and maple flavoring. Beat at low speed of electric mixer till combined, then at high speed about 5 minutes or till satin smooth. Stir in chopped walnuts.

Thoroughly wash beaters. In a large mixing bowl beat egg whites and cream of tartar till stiff peaks form. Pour batter in a thin stream over entire surface of egg whites; fold in lightly by hand. Turn into an *ungreased* 10-inch tube pan. Bake in a 325° oven for 65 to 70 minutes or till done. Invert cake in pan; cool thoroughly. Loosen cake; remove from pan. Just before serving, frost with sweetened whipped cream and garnish with additional chopped nuts or halved strawberries, if desired. Makes 12 servings.

Dress up *Chocolate Chiffon Cake* (see recipe, page 30): Split and fill with
Vanilla Cream Filling, then frost in 'web' pattern. See *Frostings and Fillings* chapter for hints.

Golden Chiffon Cake   (chocolate variation pictured on page 29; marble variation pictured on cover)

2¼ **cups sifted cake flour** *or* **2 cups**
     all-purpose flour
1½ **cups sugar**
 1 **tablespoon baking powder**
 1 **teaspoon salt**
½   **cup cooking oil**
 7 **egg yolks**
¾   **cup cold water**
 2 **teaspoons finely shredded**
     lemon peel
 1 **teaspoon vanilla**
 7 **egg whites**
½   **teaspoon cream of tartar**

In a large mixer bowl sift together cake or all-purpose flour, sugar, baking powder, and salt. Make a well in the center. Add cooking oil, egg yolks, water, lemon peel, and vanilla. Beat at low speed of electric mixer till combined, then at high speed about 5 minutes or till satin smooth.

Thoroughly wash beaters. In a large mixing bowl beat egg whites and cream of tartar till stiff peaks form. Pour batter in a thin stream over entire surface of egg whites; fold in lightly by hand. Turn into an *ungreased* 10-inch tube pan. Bake in a 325° oven for 65 to 70 minutes or till done. Invert cake in pan; cool thoroughly. Loosen cake; remove from pan. Serves 12.

Chocolate Chiffon Cake: In a small saucepan combine 4 squares (4 ounces) *unsweetened chocolate*, cut up; ½ cup *water*; and ¼ cup *sugar*. Heat and stir over low heat till chocolate is melted and mixture is smooth; cool. Prepare Golden Chiffon Cake as above *except* stir chocolate mixture into beaten egg yolk mixture; omit lemon peel. If desired, split cake horizontally into 3 layers; spread Vanilla Cream Filling between layers (see recipe, page 52). Spread Chocolate Icing over top, drizzling down sides. Immediately drizzle Powdered Sugar Icing around top. (See recipes, page 52.) Before icing has set, draw knife through icing at regular intervals to give web effect.

Marble Chiffon Cake: In a small saucepan combine 2 squares (2 ounces) *unsweetened chocolate*, cut up; ¼ cup *water*; and 2 tablespoons *sugar*. Heat and stir over low heat till chocolate is melted and mixture is smooth; cool. Prepare Golden Chiffon Cake as above *except* omit lemon peel. Fold yolk mixture into beaten egg whites. Remove ⅓ of the batter to a separate bowl; gently fold in chocolate mixture. Turn *half* the light batter into an *ungreased* 10-inch tube pan; top with *half* the dark batter. Repeat layers of light and dark batters. With narrow spatula, swirl gently through batters to marble, leaving definite light and dark areas. Bake as directed. If desired, frost top with Cream Cheese Icing, drizzling down sides (see recipe, page 52).

Tropical Chiffon Cake: Prepare Golden Chiffon Cake as above *except* substitute ¾ cup *orange juice* for ¾ cup cold water; stir 1⅓ cups *flaked coconut* into beaten yolk mixture.

Grapefruit Chiffon Cake

2¼ **cups sifted cake flour** *or* **2 cups**
     all-purpose flour
1½ **cups sugar**
 1 **tablespoon baking powder**
 1 **teaspoon salt**
½   **cup cooking oil**
 5 **egg yolks**
 1 **tablespoon finely shredded**
     grapefruit peel
⅔   **cup grapefruit juice**
 8 **egg whites**
½   **teaspoon cream of tartar**

In a large mixer bowl sift together cake or all-purpose flour, sugar, baking powder, and salt. Make a well in the center. Add cooking oil, egg yolks, grapefruit peel, and juice. Beat at low speed of electric mixer till combined, then at high speed about 5 minutes or till satin smooth. Thoroughly wash beaters. In a large mixing bowl beat egg whites and cream of tartar till stiff peaks form. Pour batter in a thin stream over entire surface of egg whites; fold in lightly by hand. Turn into an *ungreased* 10-inch tube pan. Bake in a 325° oven for 65 to 70 minutes or till cake tests done. Invert cake in pan; cool thoroughly. Loosen cake; remove from pan. Makes 12 servings.

Cake Rolls

A cake roll is a thin sponge cake rolled around a filling. Jelly is the traditional filling for this dessert, but you can serve cake rolls filled with pudding, pie filling, whipped cream (plain or with fruit), or softened ice cream.

*P*repare batter and bake until cake springs back and leaves no imprint when lightly touched. Using a narrow spatula, loosen edges at once. Holding pan with pot holders, quickly invert and shake gently over a towel sprinkled with sifted powdered sugar (the powdered sugar helps keep the warm cake from sticking to towel). Carefully lift off pan.

*S*tarting with the narrow end, roll the warm cake and the towel together, as shown. It's necessary to roll the cake while it's still warm to prevent tearing. The towel keeps the cake from sticking together as it cools.

Place cake roll on a wire rack to cool thoroughly.

*C*arefully unroll the cooled cake and the towel. Spoon desired filling onto cake and spread over the surface to within 1 inch of edges. Again starting with narrow end, roll up only the cake. If desired, trim ends. Place cake on serving platter, seam side down. If necessary, refrigerate or freeze till serving time. To serve, slice crosswise into 1-inch slices.

Jelly Roll

½ **cup all-purpose flour**
1 **teaspoon baking powder**
¼ **teaspoon salt**
4 **egg yolks**
½ **teaspoon vanilla**
⅓ **cup sugar**
4 **egg whites**
½ **cup sugar**
   Sifted powdered sugar
½ **cup jelly *or* jam**

Grease and lightly flour a 15x10x1-inch jelly roll pan; set aside. Stir together flour, baking powder, and salt. In a small mixer bowl beat egg yolks and vanilla at high speed of electric mixer about 5 minutes or till thick and lemon-colored. Gradually add the ⅓ cup sugar, beating till sugar dissolves. Thoroughly wash beaters.

In a large mixer bowl beat egg whites at medium speed till soft peaks form. Gradually add the ½ cup sugar; continue beating at high speed till stiff peaks form. Fold yolk mixture into egg whites. Sprinkle flour mixture over egg mixture; fold in lightly by hand. Spread batter evenly into pan. Bake in a 375° oven for 12 to 15 minutes or till done. Immediately loosen edges of cake from pan and turn out onto a towel sprinkled with sifted powdered sugar. Starting with narrow end, roll warm cake and towel together; cool on a wire rack. Unroll; spread cake with jelly or jam to within 1 inch of edges. Roll up cake. Makes 10 servings.

Before baking *Pumpkin Cake Roll*, sprinkle chopped walnuts over
the batter to give the cream cheese-filled cake its attractive, rough covering.

Lincoln Log

½ cup all-purpose flour
¼ cup unsweetened cocoa
   powder
1 teaspoon baking powder
¼ teaspoon salt
4 egg yolks
½ teaspoon vanilla
⅓ cup sugar
4 egg whites
½ cup sugar
   Sifted powdered sugar
1 cup whipping cream
   Chocolate Glaze (see recipe,
   page 12)

Grease and lightly flour a 15x10x1-inch jelly roll pan; set aside. *Sift* together flour, cocoa powder, baking powder, and salt. In a small mixer bowl beat egg yolks and vanilla at high speed of electric mixer about 5 minutes or till thick and lemon-colored. Gradually add the ⅓ cup sugar, beating till sugar dissolves. Thoroughly wash beaters.

In a large mixer bowl beat egg whites at medium speed till soft peaks form. Gradually add the ½ cup sugar; continue beating at high speed till stiff peaks form. Fold yolk mixture into egg whites. Sprinkle flour-cocoa mixture over egg mixture; fold in lightly by hand. Spread batter evenly into prepared pan. Bake in a 375° oven for 12 to 15 minutes or till cake tests done.

Immediately loosen edges of cake from pan and turn out onto a towel sprinkled with sifted powdered sugar. Starting with narrow end, roll warm cake and the towel together; cool on a wire rack. Beat whipping cream till stiff peaks form. Unroll cake; spread with whipped cream. Roll up cake only. Frost with hot Chocolate Glaze, drizzling down sides. If desired, garnish with toasted sliced almonds. Chill till serving time. Makes 10 servings.

Peppermint Ice Cream Roll: Prepare and bake cake for Lincoln Log as directed above. Roll warm cake and the towel together; cool. Soften 1 quart *peppermint ice cream* by stirring and pressing it against sides of a bowl just till pliable. Unroll cake; spread with softened ice cream. Roll up cake only; freeze. To serve, stir ¼ cup crushed *peppermint candy* into ½ of a 4-ounce container frozen whipped *dessert topping,* thawed. Spread mixture over top and sides of cake. (If desired, store cake in freezer as long as 1 hour before serving.) Garnish with additional crushed *peppermint candy.*

Pumpkin Cake Roll

¾ cup all-purpose flour
2 teaspoons ground cinnamon
1 teaspoon baking powder
1 teaspoon ground ginger
½ teaspoon salt
½ teaspoon ground nutmeg
3 eggs
1 cup sugar
⅔ cup canned pumpkin
1 teaspoon lemon juice
1 cup chopped walnuts
   Sifted powdered sugar
2 3-ounce packages cream
   cheese
¼ cup butter *or* margarine
½ teaspoon vanilla
1 cup sifted powdered sugar

Grease and lightly flour a 15x10x1-inch jelly roll pan; set aside. Stir together flour, cinnamon, baking powder, ginger, salt, and nutmeg. In a small mixer bowl beat *whole* eggs at high speed of electric mixer about 5 minutes or till thick and lemon-colored. Gradually add sugar, beating till sugar dissolves. Stir in pumpkin and lemon juice. Fold dry ingredients into pumpkin mixture. Spread evenly into prepared pan. Sprinkle with walnuts. Bake in a 375° oven for 12 to 15 minutes or till done.

Immediately loosen edges of cake from pan and turn out onto a towel sprinkled with sifted powdered sugar. Starting with narrow end, roll warm cake and the towel together, nuts on outside of roll. Cool on a wire rack. For filling, beat cream cheese, butter or margarine, and vanilla till smooth. Beat in 1 cup powdered sugar. Unroll cake; spread with filling. Roll up cake only; chill till serving time. Makes 10 servings.

Pound Cakes & Fruitcakes

Dark Fruitcake (See recipe, page 39.)

Pound Cakes

Rich, moist, and compact, pound cakes are often baked in loaf or tube pans. Serve plain or with butter, a sauce, or a topping. You can layer pound cake cubes with pudding, and revive stale pound cake by soaking in wine or toasting slices.

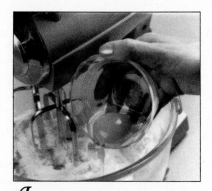

*W*hen preparing a pound cake, in mixer bowl beat softened butter on medium speed of electric mixer till fluffy, as shown. Use a rubber spatula to guide the butter toward the beaters for thorough creaming. Gradually add sugar, beating on medium speed till light and fluffy. Scrape the bowl frequently.

*A*dd the eggs to the creamed mixture, one at a time, beating about 1 minute after each addition. Scrape the bowl frequently and guide the mixture toward the beaters for thorough mixing. After adding and beating in the eggs, the cake batter will have a fluffy but somewhat curdled appearance.

*S*pread the batter evenly in the prepared pan; bake as directed. To test pound cake for doneness, insert a wooden pick in the center of the baked cake. If wooden pick comes out clean and dry, the cake is done. Set cake on wire rack to cool for 10 minutes before removing from pan. Cool completely.

Pound Cake

Pound cakes were so named because they originally were made with a pound each of butter, sugar, eggs, and flour —

- **1 cup butter *or* margarine**
- **4 eggs**
- **2 cups all-purpose flour**
- **1 teaspoon baking powder**
- **¼ teaspoon salt**
- **¼ teaspoon ground nutmeg**
- **1 cup sugar**
- **1½ teaspoons vanilla**

Bring butter and eggs to room temperature. Grease and flour a 9x5x3-inch loaf pan. Stir together flour, baking powder, salt, and nutmeg. In mixer bowl beat butter with electric mixer till fluffy. Gradually add sugar, beating till fluffy. Add eggs, one at a time, beating 1 minute after each; scrape bowl frequently. Stir in vanilla. Gradually add dry ingredients to beaten mixture, beating just till well blended. Turn batter into pan. Bake in a 325° oven for 55 to 65 minutes or till done. Cool 10 minutes on a wire rack. Remove from pan; cool. Makes 12 servings.

Mocha Pound Cake: Prepare Pound Cake as directed above *except* add 1 tablespoon instant *coffee crystals* with the vanilla. After beating in eggs, stir in 2 squares (2 ounces) *unsweetened chocolate*, melted and cooled.

Currant Pound Cake: In small bowl combine ½ cup *dried currants* and 2 tablespoons *brandy*. Cover tightly and let stand at room temperature for several hours or overnight; drain. Prepare Pound Cake as directed above *except* fold drained currants into batter before baking.

Sour Cream Pound Cake

1 **cup butter or margarine**
6 **eggs**
3 **cups all-purpose flour**
½ **teaspoon salt**
¼ **teaspoon baking soda**
2¾ **cups sugar**
½ **teaspoon lemon extract**
½ **teaspoon orange extract**
½ **teaspoon vanilla**
1 **cup dairy sour cream**
Powdered sugar (optional)

Bring butter or margarine and eggs to room temperature. Grease and flour a 10-inch tube pan. Stir together flour, salt, and baking soda. In mixer bowl beat butter or margarine on medium speed of electric mixer till fluffy. Gradually add sugar, beating till light and fluffy.

Add eggs, one at a time, beating 1 minute after each; scrape bowl frequently, guiding mixture toward beaters. Add lemon extract, orange extract, and vanilla; beat well. Add dry ingredients and sour cream alternately to beaten mixture, beating after each addition just till combined. Turn batter into prepared pan. Bake in a 350° oven about 1½ hours or till done. Cool 15 minutes on wire rack. Remove from pan; cool. Sift powdered sugar over cake, if desired. Makes 16 servings.

Marble Pound Cake

¾ **cup butter *or* margarine**
3 **eggs**
½ **cup milk**
2 **cups all-purpose flour**
1 **teaspoon baking powder**
¼ **teaspoon salt**
1¼ **cups sugar**
1 **teaspoon finely shredded lemon peel**
1 **tablespoon lemon juice**
1 **square (1 ounce) unsweetened chocolate, melted and cooled**
2 **tablespoons boiling water**
1 **tablespoon sugar**
¼ **teaspoon ground cinnamon**
Powdered sugar (optional)

Bring butter, eggs, and milk to room temperature. Grease a 9x5x3-inch loaf pan. Stir together flour, baking powder, and salt. In mixer bowl beat butter on medium speed of electric mixer till fluffy. Gradually add 1¼ cups sugar, beating till fluffy. Add eggs, one at a time, beating 1 minute after each; scrape bowl often. Add milk, lemon peel, and juice; beat on low speed till blended. Gradually add dry ingredients to beaten mixture, beating on low speed just till smooth.

Divide batter in half. Combine chocolate, boiling water, 1 tablespoon sugar, and cinnamon; stir into half of the batter. In pan alternate spoonfuls of light and dark batters. Using a narrow spatula, stir gently through batter to marble. Bake in a 325° oven about 70 minutes or till done. Cool 10 minutes on wire rack. Remove from pan; cool. Sift powdered sugar over cake, if desired. Makes 12 servings.

Chocolate Torte

Pound Cake (see recipe, page 35) *or* 1 frozen loaf pound cake
4 **squares (4 ounces) semisweet chocolate**
1 **15-ounce container ricotta cheese (about 2 cups)**
½ **cup sugar**
1½ **teaspoons vanilla**
6 **tablespoons Amaretto, orange liqueur, *or* crème de cacao**
1 **cup sifted powdered sugar**
2 **tablespoons unsweetened cocoa powder**
1 **tablespoon butter, melted**
2 **to 3 tablespoons boiling water**
2 **tablespoons chopped walnuts**

Let pound cake stand at room temperature, if frozen. Meanwhile, finely chop chocolate squares. For filling, in bowl combine chopped chocolate, ricotta cheese, sugar, and vanilla. Slice pound cake horizontally into 3 layers. Drizzle *2 tablespoons* of the liqueur over one side of *each* cake layer. Set aside 2 tablespoons ricotta filling. Divide remaining filling in half; spread mixture evenly on the liqueur side of 2 of the cake layers. Stack the cake layers with filling; top with remaining cake layer.

In mixing bowl stir together powdered sugar and cocoa powder; stir in melted butter. Stir in enough boiling water to make of glazing consistency. Spread mixture over top, drizzling down sides. Dollop the reserved ricotta filling atop cake; sprinkle with walnuts. Chill. Store in refrigerator. Makes 12 servings.

Easily turn a homemade or purchased frozen pound cake into
this *Chocolate Torte* by dressing it up with ricotta cheese, chocolate, and liqueur.

Fruitcakes

Fruitcakes are rich cakes filled with the treasures of nuts and dried or candied fruits and peels. It's a traditional holiday cake, but you can serve it year-round. Unlike most cakes, a fruitcake's flavor and texture improve with age.

*W*hen preparing the fruitcake batter, thoroughly combine the nuts, fruits, and peels with the other ingredients, separating the pieces of fruit so they are evenly distributed.

*G*rease pans; line pan bottoms and sides with strips of brown paper. Grease the paper. Using a measuring cup, spoon batter into prepared pans, filling each about ¾ full. Use a rubber spatula to distribute the batter evenly. Bake until a wooden pick inserted in center of cake comes out clean and dry.

*W*rap each baked and cooled cake in several layers of wine-, brandy-, or fruit juice-moistened cheesecloth. Overwrap each cake with foil. Store in refrigerator for a blended and mellow flavor. Remoisten cheesecloth with wine, brandy, or fruit juice once a week.

Light Fruitcake

      3 **cups all-purpose flour**
      1 **teaspoon baking powder**
      1 **cup butter *or* margarine**
      1 **cup sugar**
      4 **eggs**
      ½ **cup orange juice***
      ¼ **cup light corn syrup**
      1 **teaspoon lemon extract**
     12 **ounces whole red *or* green candied cherries (2 cups)**
      8 **ounces diced mixed candied fruits and peels (1¼ cups)**
      1 **cup light raisins**
      1 **cup chopped candied pineapple**
      1 **cup chopped walnuts**

Grease one 5½-cup ring mold and six 4½x2½x1½-inch individual loaf pans (*or* one 5½-cup ring mold and one 10x3½x2½-inch loaf dessert pan). Stir together flour and baking powder. In mixer bowl beat butter about 30 seconds. Add sugar and beat till fluffy. Add eggs, one at a time, beating 1 minute after each. Combine orange juice, corn syrup, and lemon extract. Add dry ingredients and orange juice mixture alternately to beaten mixture, beating after each addition. Combine cherries, mixed fruits and peels, raisins, pineapple, and nuts; fold into batter. Turn into pans.

Bake in a 300° oven for 50 to 60 minutes (70 minutes for larger loaf pan) or till done. Cool on wire racks. Remove from pans. Wrap in wine-, brandy-, or fruit juice-moistened cheesecloth. Overwrap with foil or clear plastic wrap, or place in an airtight container. Store in the refrigerator at least 1 week. Remoisten cheesecloth as needed if cakes are stored more than 1 week.

*Note: If desired, use ¼ *cup* orange juice and ¼ cup dry *white wine* instead of the ½ cup orange juice.

Dark Fruitcake (pictured on page 34)

¾ cup butter *or* margarine
3 cups all-purpose flour
2 teaspoons baking powder
2 teaspoons ground cinnamon
½ teaspoon *each* ground nutmeg,
   allspice, and cloves
16 ounces diced mixed candied
   fruits and peels (2½ cups)
1 15-ounce package raisins
1 8-ounce package (1⅓ cups)
   pitted whole dates, snipped
8 ounces whole red *or* green
   candied cherries (1⅓ cups)
1 cup slivered almonds
1 cup pecan halves
½ cup chopped candied pineapple
4 eggs
1¾ cups packed brown sugar
1 cup orange juice
¼ cup light molasses

Grease three 8x4x2-inch loaf pans or two 10x3½x2½-inch loaf dessert pans. Line bottom and sides of pans with brown paper to prevent overbrowning; grease paper. In saucepan melt butter or margarine; cool. Stir together flour, baking powder, cinnamon, nutmeg, allspice, cloves, and 1 teaspoon *salt*. Add mixed fruits and peels, raisins, dates, cherries, almonds, pecans, and pineapple; mix till well coated. Beat eggs till foamy. Add brown sugar, orange juice, molasses, and butter or margarine; beat till blended. Stir into fruit mixture.

Turn batter into prepared pans, filling each about ¾ full. Bake in a 300° oven about 2 hours or till cakes test done. (Cover all pans loosely with foil after 1 hour of baking to prevent overbrowning.) Place cakes on wire racks; cool thoroughly. Remove from pans. Wrap in wine-, brandy-, or fruit juice-moistened cheesecloth. Overwrap with foil. Store in the refrigerator for 3 to 4 weeks before serving. Remoisten the cheesecloth once a week.

Last-Minute Fruitcake

2½ cups all-purpose flour
1 teaspoon baking soda
¼ teaspoon *each* ground
   cinnamon, cloves, and
   nutmeg
½ cup shortening
¾ cup sugar
1 egg
1 teaspoon instant coffee crystals
1 cup applesauce
2 cups diced mixed candied
   fruits and peels
1 cup raisins
1 cup chopped nuts

Grease and lightly flour two 8x4x2-inch loaf pans. Stir together flour, baking soda, cinnamon, cloves, nutmeg, and 1 teaspoon *salt*. In mixer bowl beat shortening on medium speed of electric mixer about 30 seconds. Add sugar and beat till fluffy. Add egg; beat well. Dissolve coffee crystals in ¼ cup *water*; stir in applesauce. Add dry ingredients and applesauce mixture alternately to beaten mixture, beating on low speed after each addition just till combined. Fold in mixed fruits and peels, raisins, and nuts.

Turn batter into prepared pans. Bake in 325° oven for 1 to 1¼ hours or till cakes test done. Place cakes on wire racks; cool for 10 minutes. Remove from pans; cool. If desired, wrap in wine-moistened cheesecloth. Overwrap with foil. Store in refrigerator at least 24 hours.

Cranberry Nut Fruitcake

1½ cups coarsely chopped filberts
   or almonds
1½ cups chopped cranberries
1 8-ounce package chopped
   pitted dates
1 cup walnut halves
¾ cup sugar
¾ cup all-purpose flour
½ teaspoon baking powder
½ teaspoon ground mace
3 eggs
1 teaspoon vanilla

Grease a 9x5x3-inch loaf pan. Line with brown paper; grease. In large mixing bowl combine filberts, cranberries, dates, and walnuts. Stir together sugar, flour, baking powder, mace, and ½ teaspoon *salt*. Beat eggs and vanilla till foamy. Stir in dry ingredients; pour over fruit mixture, stirring to mix well. Turn into pan. Cover with foil. Bake in 300° oven for 20 minutes. Remove foil. Bake about 1 hour 40 minutes more or till done. Cool on wire rack. Remove from pan. Wrap in wine-, brandy-, or fruit juice-moistened cheesecloth. Overwrap with foil. Store in refrigerator at least 1 week. Do not remoisten.

Start with Cake Mix

Chocolate Date Cake (pictured on pages 4 and 5)

1¼ cups boiling water
1 8-ounce package (1½ cups) pitted whole dates, snipped
1 package 2-layer-size chocolate cake mix
1 6-ounce package (1 cup) semisweet chocolate pieces
½ cup chopped walnuts
Vanilla ice cream (optional)

Grease and lightly flour a 13x9x2-inch baking pan; set aside. Pour boiling water over dates; cool. Prepare cake mix according to package directions *except* substitute date mixture for the liquid. Turn batter into prepared pan. Top evenly with chocolate pieces and nuts. Bake in a 350° oven for 35 to 40 minutes or till cake tests done. Serve with ice cream, if desired. Makes 12 servings.

Cherry Devilicious Cake

1 teaspoon ground cinnamon
½ teaspoon ground nutmeg
1 package 2-layer-size devil's food cake mix
1 8-ounce package cream cheese, softened
2 tablespoons sugar
2 tablespoons milk
1 1½-ounce envelope dessert topping mix
1 16-ounce can pitted dark sweet cherries
2 tablespoons cornstarch
2 tablespoons sugar
¼ cup water
¼ cup burgundy

Grease a 10-inch fluted tube pan. Stir cinnamon and nutmeg into dry cake mix; prepare mix according to package directions. Turn batter into prepared pan. Bake in a 350° oven for 40 to 45 minutes or till cake tests done. Place cake on wire rack; cool for 10 minutes. Remove from pan; cool thoroughly. If desired, sift with powdered sugar before serving.

In mixing bowl beat together cream cheese, 2 tablespoons sugar, and the milk till fluffy. Prepare topping mix according to package directions; fold into cream cheese mixture. Cover and chill. Drain cherries, reserving syrup. In a small saucepan stir together cornstarch and 2 tablespoons sugar. Gradually stir in the reserved cherry syrup and the water. Cook and stir till thickened and bubbly. Cook 1 minute longer. Stir in cherries; heat through. Remove from heat; stir in burgundy. Spoon cherry sauce and cream cheese mixture over cake slices. Makes 12 servings.

Spicy Pumpkin Cake

1 package 2-layer-size yellow cake mix
1 8½-ounce can applesauce
1 cup canned pumpkin
3 eggs
¼ cup milk
1½ teaspoons ground cinnamon
½ teaspoon ground nutmeg
¼ teaspoon ground cloves
½ cup finely chopped, peeled apple
½ cup chopped nuts
1 cup whipping cream
2 tablespoons honey
¼ teaspoon ground cinnamon

Grease and lightly flour a 13x9x2-inch baking pan; set aside. In mixer bowl combine cake mix, applesauce, pumpkin, eggs, milk, 1½ teaspoons cinnamon, nutmeg, and cloves; beat on low speed of electric mixer till well blended. Beat on medium speed for 2 minutes, scraping sides of bowl frequently. Fold in chopped apple and nuts.

Turn batter into prepared pan. Bake in a 350° oven for 35 to 40 minutes or till done. Place cake on wire rack; cool thoroughly. Combine whipping cream, honey, and the ¼ teaspoon cinnamon; beat till soft peaks form. Cut cake into squares; top with whipped cream. Makes 12 servings.

Elegant—and enticing—*Cherry Devilicious Cake* starts with a devil's food cake mix.
Serve this easy dessert with a cherry-burgundy sauce and fluffy cream cheese topping.

Orange Honey Cake

1 package 2-layer-size yellow
  cake mix
¾ cup water
1 teaspoon finely shredded
  orange peel
½ cup orange juice
2 eggs
¼ cup honey
  Orange Butter Frosting (see
  recipe, page 50)

Generously grease and lightly flour two 9x1½-inch round baking pans; set aside. In mixing bowl combine cake mix, water, orange peel, orange juice, eggs, and honey; beat for 3 minutes. Turn batter into prepared pans.

Bake in a 350° oven for 30 to 35 minutes or till cakes test done. Place cakes on wire racks; cool for 10 minutes. Remove from pans; cool thoroughly on racks. Fill and frost with Orange Butter Frosting. Makes 12 servings.

Blueberry Lemon Cake

1½ cups fresh *or* frozen
  unsweetened blueberries
1 package 2-layer-size lemon
  cake mix
1 8-ounce carton lemon yogurt
4 eggs
  Cinnamon Blueberry Sauce (see
  recipe, page 53)

Grease and lightly flour a 10-inch tube pan or fluted tube pan; set aside. Thaw blueberries, if frozen. Rinse fresh or thawed, frozen berries; drain well. In a large mixer bowl combine cake mix, yogurt, and eggs. Beat on low speed of electric mixer till combined, then on medium speed for 2 minutes. By hand, fold in berries.

Turn batter into prepared pan. Bake in a 350° oven about 45 minutes or till cake tests done. Place cake on wire rack; cool for 10 minutes. Remove from pan; cool thoroughly. Spoon Cinnamon Blueberry Sauce over cake slices. Serves 12.

Easy Pound Cake

1 package 2-layer-size yellow
  cake mix
1 1½-ounce envelope dessert
  topping mix
1 cup water
4 eggs
1 1½-ounce envelope dessert
  topping mix
  Strawberry Sauce (see recipe,
  page 53)

Grease and lightly flour a 10-inch tube pan or fluted tube pan; set aside. In a large mixer bowl combine cake mix, 1 envelope dessert topping mix, water, and eggs. Beat on low speed of electric mixer till blended, then on medium speed for 4 minutes. Turn batter into prepared pan. Bake in a 350° oven about 45 minutes or till cake tests done. Place cake on wire rack; cool for 10 minutes. Remove from pan; cool thoroughly on rack.

To serve, prepare remaining envelope topping mix according to package directions; stir in enough additional milk to make spoonable. Serve Strawberry Sauce over cake slices; garnish with whipped topping. Makes 12 servings.

Cream Cheese-Filled Cupcakes

1 8-ounce package cream cheese,
  softened
⅓ cup sugar
1 egg
  Dash salt
1 6-ounce package (1 cup)
  semisweet chocolate pieces
1 package 2-layer-size chocolate
  cake mix

In small mixer bowl beat cream cheese and sugar on medium speed of electric mixer till fluffy; beat in egg and salt. Stir in chocolate pieces; set aside.

Prepare chocolate cake mix according to package directions. Line muffin pans with paper bake cups; fill ⅔ full. Drop 1 well rounded teaspoonful cream cheese mixture into each bake cup. Bake in a 350° oven about 20 minutes or till done. Makes 32 cupcakes.

Coconut Spice Cake Ring

3 tablespoons butter *or*
   margarine
⅓ cup packed brown sugar
2 tablespoons light corn syrup
1 tablespoon water
⅔ cup coconut
1 package 1-layer-size spice
   cake mix
   Vanilla ice cream *or* whipped
   cream (optional)

In a small saucepan melt butter or margarine; remove from heat. Stir in brown sugar, corn syrup, and water. Pour into an ungreased 5½-cup oven-proof ring mold; sprinkle with coconut. Prepare cake mix according to package directions; pour over coconut. Bake in a 350° oven for 25 to 30 minutes or till cake tests done.

Immediately loosen sides and invert cake onto a serving plate; remove mold. Serve warm with vanilla ice cream or whipped cream, if desired. Makes 8 servings.

Crunchy Apricot Cake

Next time try a different combination of pie filling and cake mix: cherry filling with chocolate cake, strawberry filling with white cake, or apple filling with spice cake —

1 21-ounce can apricot pie filling
1 package 1-layer-size yellow
   cake mix
½ cup coconut
½ cup chopped pecans
¼ cup butter *or* margarine, melted

Spread pie filling in the bottom of a 9x9x2-inch baking pan. Prepare cake mix according to package directions. Pour batter over pie filling; sprinkle with coconut and chopped pecans. Drizzle with melted butter or margarine. Bake in a 350° oven about 40 minutes or till cake tests done. Serve warm. Makes 9 servings.

Peanut Butter-Topped Cake

1 package 2-layer-size yellow
   cake mix
1 cup packed brown sugar
⅓ cup peanut butter
2 tablespoons butter *or*
   margarine
¼ cup milk
1⅓ cups coconut

Grease and lightly flour a 13x9x2-inch baking pan; set aside. Prepare cake mix according to package directions. Turn batter into prepared pan. Bake in a 350° oven for 30 to 35 minutes or till cake tests done.

Meanwhile, in mixing bowl beat brown sugar, peanut butter, and butter or margarine till fluffy. Blend in milk; stir in coconut. Spread mixture over warm cake in pan. Broil 4 to 5 inches from heat for 2 to 3 minutes or till golden brown. Serve warm. Makes 12 servings.

Fudge Pudding Cake

1 package 1-layer-size chocolate
   cake mix
2½ cups water
1 tablespoon instant coffee
   crystals
1 package 4-serving-size *regular*
   chocolate pudding mix
   Whipped cream

Grease and lightly flour a 9x9x2-inch baking pan; set aside. Prepare cake mix according to package directions. Turn batter into prepared pan.

Stir together water and instant coffee crystals; gradually stir into pudding mix. Pour evenly over cake batter. Bake in a 350° oven for 40 to 45 minutes or till cake tests done. Serve warm with whipped cream. Makes 9 servings.

Lemon Pound Cake (pictured on pages 4 and 5)

1   **package 2-layer-size yellow cake mix**
1   **package 4-serving-size *instant* lemon pudding mix**
¾   **cup water**
¼   **cup cooking oil**
4   **eggs**
2   **cups sifted powdered sugar**
⅓   **cup lemon juice**
    Thin lemon slices (optional)

Grease and lightly flour a 10-inch tube pan or fluted tube pan; set aside. In a large mixer bowl combine yellow cake mix, lemon pudding mix, water, cooking oil, and eggs. Beat on low speed of electric mixer till mixture is combined, then on medium speed for 2 minutes.

Pour batter into prepared pan. Bake in a 350° oven for 45 to 50 minutes or till cake tests done. Place cake on wire rack; cool for 10 minutes. Place waxed paper under wire rack. Remove cake from pan; place on wire rack over waxed paper.

Meanwhile, for syrup: In a small saucepan combine sifted powdered sugar and lemon juice; bring to boiling. Prick holes in the top of cake with tines of a fork. Spoon syrup slowly over top and down sides of cake, allowing the syrup to soak in. Cool cake thoroughly. If desired, garnish with thin lemon slices. Makes 12 servings.

Butterscotch Marble Cake

1   **package 2-layer-size white cake mix**
1   **package 4-serving-size *instant* butterscotch pudding mix**
1   **cup water**
¼   **cup cooking oil**
4   **eggs**
½   **cup chocolate-flavored syrup**
½   **recipe Chocolate Icing (see recipe, page 52)**

Grease and lightly flour a 10-inch fluted tube pan; set aside. In a large mixer bowl combine white cake mix, butterscotch pudding mix, water, cooking oil, and eggs.

Beat on low speed of electric mixer till mixture is combined, then on medium speed for 2 minutes. Set aside 1½ cups of the batter. Turn the remaining batter into the prepared pan. Stir together the reserved 1½ cups batter and the chocolate-flavored syrup.

Pour chocolate mixture over batter in pan. With a narrow spatula, swirl gently through the batters to marble. Bake in a 350° oven about 60 minutes or till cake tests done. Place cake on wire rack; cool for 10 minutes. Remove from pan; cool thoroughly on rack. Glaze cake with Chocolate Icing. Makes 12 servings.

Granola Ripple Cake

1   **package 2-layer-size white cake mix**
1   **package 4-serving-size *instant* butterscotch pudding mix**
1   **cup water**
¼   **cup cooking oil**
4   **eggs**
2   **cups granola**
    Powdered sugar

Grease and lightly flour a 10-inch fluted tube pan; set aside. In a large mixer bowl combine white cake mix, butterscotch pudding mix, water, cooking oil, and eggs. Beat on low speed of electric mixer till mixture is combined, then on medium speed for 2 minutes.

Turn ¾ of the batter into the prepared pan. Sprinkle with granola. Spoon the remaining batter over granola layer. Bake in a 350° oven about 50 minutes or till cake tests done. Place cake on wire rack; cool for 10 minutes. Remove from pan; cool thoroughly on wire rack. Sift powdered sugar over cake. Makes 12 servings.

Granola adds a crunchy layer to *Granola Ripple Cake*. A dusting
of powdered sugar gives an extra, light touch to this moist, hearty dessert.

Sherry Spice Cake

---

1   **package 2-layer-size yellow cake mix**
1   **package 4-serving-size** *instant* **vanilla pudding mix**
¾ **cup cream sherry**
¼ **cup cooking oil**
4   **eggs**
2   **teaspoons ground nutmeg**
¼ **cup sugar**
1   **teaspoon ground cinnamon Powdered Sugar Icing (see recipe, page 52)**

Grease and lightly flour a 10-inch fluted tube pan; set aside. In large mixer bowl combine cake mix, pudding mix, sherry, cooking oil, eggs, and nutmeg. Beat on low speed of electric mixer till combined, then on medium speed for 2 minutes. Pour ⅓ of the batter into prepared pan.

Stir together sugar and cinnamon; sprinkle *half* of the sugar mixture over batter in pan. Add another ⅓ of the batter and sprinkle with the remaining sugar mixture. Top with the remaining batter. Bake in a 350° oven for 40 to 45 minutes or till cake tests done. Place cake on wire rack; cool for 10 minutes. Remove from pan; cool thoroughly on rack. Glaze with Powdered Sugar Icing (use cream sherry instead of milk, if desired). Makes 12 servings.

Date Nut Squares

---

1   **package 2-layer-size white cake mix**
1   **package 4-serving-size** *instant* **coconut cream** *or* **vanilla pudding mix**
¼ **cup butter, softened**
3   **eggs**
½ **cup all-purpose flour**
⅓ **cup packed brown sugar**
1   **teaspoon vanilla**
1   **8-ounce package (1½ cups) pitted whole dates, snipped**
½ **cup chopped walnuts**

Grease a 13x9x2-inch baking pan; set aside. In mixer bowl combine cake mix, coconut cream or vanilla pudding mix, butter, and 1 of the eggs. Beat on low speed of electric mixer about 1 minute or till crumbly. Set aside ¾ cup crumb mixture. Press remaining crumb mixture into bottom of prepared pan. Bake in a 350° oven for 15 minutes.

Meanwhile, in same bowl combine flour, brown sugar, vanilla, the remaining 2 eggs, ¼ cup *water*, and ⅛ teaspoon *salt*; beat till smooth. Stir in dates and nuts; carefully spread over baked layer. Sprinkle with reserved ¾ cup crumb mixture. Bake in 350° oven 20 to 25 minutes. Cool. Cut into squares. Serve with whipped cream, if desired. Serves 12.

Apple Upside-Down Cake

---

1   **large tart cooking apple**
¼ **cup butter** *or* **margarine**
½ **cup honey**
½ **cup broken walnuts**
¼ **cup chopped maraschino cherries (optional)**
1   **package 1-layer-size spice** *or* **yellow cake mix**

Core unpeeled apple and slice into ⅛-inch-thick rings. In a 10-inch oven-proof skillet melt butter or margarine. Stir in honey; add apple rings. Cook for 3 minutes, turning apples once. Remove from heat. Sprinkle with nuts and cherries. Prepare cake mix according to package directions.

Pour batter over apples. Bake in a 350° oven for 30 to 35 minutes or till done. Cool for 5 minutes in pan. Invert onto serving plate; serve warm. Makes 8 servings.

Pineapple Pound Cake

---

1   **16-ounce package pound cake mix**
⅔ **cup unsweetened pineapple juice**
2   **eggs**
½ **teaspoon ground cinnamon**
½ **cup chopped walnuts**

Grease bottom and 1 inch up sides of a 9x5x3-inch loaf pan; lightly flour pan. In small mixer bowl combine cake mix, pineapple juice, eggs, and cinnamon. Beat on low speed of electric mixer till blended. Beat on medium speed for 3 minutes, scraping bowl frequently. Fold in nuts. Turn batter into prepared pan. Bake in a 325° oven for 55 to 65 minutes or till done. Place on wire rack; cool for 10 minutes. Remove from pan; cool thoroughly. Makes 8 servings.

Spicy Angel Cake

1 teaspoon ground cinnamon
¼ teaspoon ground cloves
¼ teaspoon ground nutmeg
1 package angel cake mix
2 tablespoons instant cocoa mix
  Chocolate Icing (see recipe, page 52)

Stir cinnamon, cloves, and nutmeg into dry angel cake mix; prepare according to package directions. Turn ⅓ of the batter into an *ungreased* 10-inch tube pan; sprinkle with *half* of the instant cocoa mix. Add another ⅓ of the batter and sprinkle with the remaining cocoa mix; top with the remaining batter. Bake according to package directions. Invert cake in pan; cool thoroughly. Loosen cake; remove from pan. Frost top with Chocolate Icing, drizzling down sides. Makes 12 servings.

Burnt Sugar-Pecan Angel Cake

½ cup sugar
½ cup water
1 package angel cake mix
1 cup chopped pecans, toasted
  Burnt Sugar Icing

In a small saucepan heat sugar till melted and golden brown, stirring constantly. Stir in water; continue stirring till mixture is free of lumps. Boil without stirring for 5 to 10 minutes or till syrupy and reduced to ⅓ cup. Cool.

Prepare cake mix according to package directions *except* substitute ¼ cup of the syrup for ¼ cup water; reserve the remaining syrup for icing. Fold nuts into batter. Turn into an *ungreased* 10-inch tube pan. Bake according to package directions. Invert cake in pan; cool thoroughly. Loosen cake; remove from pan. Frost top with Burnt Sugar Icing, drizzling down sides. Makes 12 servings.

Burnt Sugar Icing: In bowl combine 1 cup sifted *powdered sugar*, 2 tablespoons softened *butter*, 2 tablespoons *milk*, and the remaining syrup from cake, beat till smooth.

Chocolate-Flecked Angel Cake

1 package angel cake mix
1 square (1 ounce) semisweet chocolate, finely shredded
  Powdered sugar (optional)

Prepare cake mix according to package directions. Fold in chocolate. Turn into an *ungreased* 10-inch tube pan. Bake according to package directions. Invert cake in pan; cool thoroughly. Loosen cake; remove from pan. Sift powdered sugar over cake, if desired. Makes 12 servings.

Holiday Fruitcake

1 package 2-layer-size yellow cake mix
½ cup orange juice
4 eggs
2 teaspoons salt
2 teaspoons lemon extract
4 cups pecan halves (16 ounces)
1 15-ounce package light raisins
8 ounces whole red *or* green candied cherries (1⅓ cups)
8 ounces candied pineapple, cut up (1⅓ cups)

Line a 10-inch tube pan (with removable bottom) with foil. Set aside ¼ cup of the cake mix. In a large mixer bowl combine remaining cake mix, orange juice, *1* of the eggs, the salt, and lemon extract; beat on medium speed of electric mixer till smooth. Add remaining eggs, one at a time, beating well after each. Combine nuts and fruits; sprinkle with the reserved ¼ cup cake mix. Mix well.

Gradually stir fruit mixture into batter, ⅓ at a time. Turn into pan; distribute evenly. Place shallow pan of water on lower oven rack. Bake cake above the pan in a 300° oven for 2 to 2½ hours or till done. Place on wire rack; cool thoroughly. Remove from pan; remove foil. Wrap in wine-, brandy-, or fruit juice-moistened cheesecloth. Overwrap with foil. Store in refrigerator for 1 week before serving.

Frostings & Fillings

Chocolate Sour Cream Frosting, Coconut Pecan Frosting, Cream Cheese Frosting, and Orange Butter Frosting (See recipes, pages 50 and 51.)

Frosting a Cake

The final touch for many cakes and cookies is a frosting, filling, or sauce. These "extras" not only create a finished look, but also add flavor. Other ways of decorating: Trim cakes or cookies with a topping or make a design in the frosting.

*C*ompletely cool a cake before frosting. For a two-layer cake, before frosting use a pastry brush or your hand to brush loose crumbs from the sides of each layer. This keeps crumbs from mixing with the frosting as you spread it. If the cake layer is too rounded on top side, it will not sit securely top side down. To steady it, use a long-bladed knife to slice a piece from the top, making it level.

*A*rrange strips of waxed paper around edge of the serving plate to keep the plate clean. Position the first cake layer, top side down, on the waxed paper-edged plate. Using a small metal spatula, spread about ¼ of the frosting over this first layer. (Or, spread a filling over the cake layer, if desired.) When using a firm frosting, such as fudge or butter frosting, spread it to the edge of the cake, as shown. When using a soft, fluffy frosting, leave about ¼ inch unfrosted a-round the edge. The weight of the second layer will cause the frosting to flow to the edge.

*P*lace the second cake layer, top side up, over the frosted layer so the edges of the layers align. This method of assembling the two layers gives the finished cake a slightly rounded top and avoids the space that results when you position the second layer top side down. If the cake top is too rounded or lopsided, use a sharp, long-bladed knife to level it by slicing off a piece. Spread the sides of the cake with a thin coat of frosting. This thin layer seals in any crumbs that may still remain. For even spreading, hold the spatula vertically, as shown.

*U*se about ⅔ of the remaining frosting to spread a thicker layer over this thin coat on the sides, making decorative swirls. Spread the remaining frosting over the top of the cake, joining the frosted sides at the edge. Swirl frosting with a spatula. Carefully remove the waxed paper strips.
    To serve cake, cut into wedges with a sharp, thin-bladed knife. Slice with an up-and-down motion, pulling the knife toward you. To prevent fluffy frosting from sticking to the knife, dip the knife in hot water before cutting the cake.

Fluffy White Frosting

1 **cup sugar**
⅓ **cup water**
¼ **teaspoon cream of tartar**
  Dash salt
2 **egg whites**
1 **teaspoon vanilla**

In a saucepan combine sugar, water, cream of tartar, and salt. Cook and stir till mixture is bubbly and sugar is dissolved. In a mixer bowl combine egg whites and vanilla. Add sugar syrup very slowly to unbeaten egg whites while beating constantly on high speed of electric mixer about 7 minutes or till stiff peaks form. Frosts tops and sides of two 8- or 9-inch layers or one 10-inch tube cake.

Butter Frosting   (variations pictured on pages 18 and 19, 48, 56, and 72 and 73)

Refrigerate or freeze any remaining frosting for another use —

6 **tablespoons butter**
4½ **to 4¾ cups sifted powdered**
    sugar
¼ **cup milk**
1½ **teaspoons vanilla**

In a small mixer bowl beat butter till light and fluffy. Gradually add about *half* of the powdered sugar, beating well. Beat in milk and vanilla. Gradually beat in remaining powdered sugar; beat in additional milk, if necessary, to make frosting of spreading consistency. Frost tops and sides of two 8- or 9-inch layers, top of one l5x10-inch pan bar cookies, about 24 cupcakes, or about 48 cookies.

Chocolate Butter Frosting: Prepare Butter Frosting as above *except* beat in 2 squares (2 ounces) *unsweetened chocolate*, melted and cooled, with the vanilla.

Orange or Lemon Butter Frosting: Prepare Butter Frosting as above *except* beat in 1 teaspoon finely shredded *orange peel* or ½ teaspoon finely shredded *lemon peel* with the vanilla. Use *orange juice or lemon juice* instead of milk.

Peanut Butter Frosting: Prepare Butter Frosting as above *except* use creamy *or* chunk-style *peanut butter* instead of the butter, and add additional milk, if necessary, to make frosting of spreading consistency.

Fudge Frosting

Beating the mixture to the proper consistency is the critical step in making Fudge Frosting. If beaten correctly, the frosting will be smooth and satiny. If not spread immediately or if overbeaten, it will soon become too stiff to spread, but can be used as fudge —

3 **cups sugar**
3 **tablespoons light corn syrup**
2 **squares (2 ounces)**
    unsweetened chocolate,
    cut up
¼ **teaspoon salt**
1 **cup milk**
¼ **cup butter *or* margarine**
1 **teaspoon vanilla**

Butter sides of a heavy 3-quart saucepan. In it combine sugar, corn syrup, chocolate, and salt; stir in milk. Cook and stir over medium heat till all the sugar dissolves and the chocolate melts. (Avoid splashing sides of pan.) Clip a candy thermometer to side of pan. Continue cooking over medium heat till thermometer registers 234° (soft-ball stage), stirring only as necessary to prevent sticking. (The mixture should boil gently over entire surface.) Watch closely: Above 220° the temperature rises quickly.

Remove from heat; add butter. Don't stir in butter; simply place it on top of mixture and let the heat of mixture melt it. Let mixture cool, without stirring, till thermometer registers 110°. (At this temperature, bottom of pan should feel comfortably warm.) Add vanilla. Using a spoon, beat mixture vigorously with an up-and-over motion for 5 to 6 minutes or till of spreading consistency. Be sure to check the consistency frequently so the frosting doesn't become too stiff. Pour and spread *immediately* atop a 13x9-inch cake. Work quickly, using a small, metal spatula to spread frosting. To smooth small areas that set up too fast, dip spatula in warm water and then smooth over these areas. Frosts top of a 13x9-inch cake.

Seven-Minute Frosting (recipe and variations pictured on pages 6, 10, and 18 and 19)

1½ cups sugar
⅓ cup cold water
2 egg whites
2 teaspoons light corn syrup *or* ¼
    teaspoon cream of tartar
  Dash salt
1 teaspoon vanilla

In the top of a double boiler combine sugar, cold water, egg whites, corn syrup or cream of tartar, and salt. Beat on low speed of electric mixer for 30 seconds to blend. Place over boiling water (upper pan should not touch water). While beating constantly on high speed of electric mixer, cook about 7 minutes or till frosting forms stiff peaks. Remove from heat; add vanilla. Beat 2 to 3 minutes longer or till of spreading consistency. Frosts tops and sides of two 8- or 9-inch layers or one 10-inch tube cake.

Seafoam Frosting: Prepare Seven-Minute Frosting as above *except* use 1½ cups packed *brown sugar* instead of sugar.

Mocha Frosting: Prepare Seven-Minute Frosting as above *except* beat in ¼ cup unsweetened *cocoa powder* and 1 teaspoon instant *coffee crystals* just before frosting cake.

Peppermint-Stick Frosting: Prepare Seven-Minute Frosting as above *except* use ¼ teaspoon *peppermint extract* instead of vanilla. Garnish cake with crushed *peppermint-stick candy,* if desired.

Chocolate Sour Cream Frosting (pictured on page 48)

1 6-ounce package (1 cup)
    semisweet chocolate pieces
¼ cup butter *or* margarine
½ cup dairy sour cream
1 teaspoon vanilla
¼ teaspoon salt
2½ cups sifted powdered sugar

In a saucepan melt chocolate pieces and butter or margarine over low heat, stirring frequently. Cool about 10 minutes. Stir in sour cream, vanilla, and salt. Gradually add powdered sugar, beating by hand till frosting is smooth and of spreading consistency. Frosts tops and sides of two 8- or 9-inch layers or about 24 cupcakes. Store, covered, in the refrigerator.

Cream Cheese Frosting (pictured on pages 4 and 5, and 48)

1 3-ounce package cream cheese
¼ cup butter *or* margarine
1 teaspoon vanilla
2 cups sifted powdered sugar
  Chopped nuts (optional)

In a mixer bowl beat together cream cheese, butter or margarine, and vanilla till light and fluffy. Gradually add powdered sugar, beating till smooth. Spread frosting over cooled cake or cookies; sprinkle with chopped nuts, if desired. Frosts tops of two 8- or 9-inch layers, top of one 13x9-inch cake or bar cookies, or about 18 cupcakes. Store, covered, in the refrigerator.

Coconut Pecan Frosting (pictured on page 48)

1 egg
⅔ cup sugar
1 5⅓-ounce can (⅔ cup)
    evaporated milk
¼ cup butter *or* margarine
  Dash salt
1 3½-ounce can (1⅓ cups) flaked
    coconut
½ cup chopped pecans

In a saucepan beat egg slightly. Stir in sugar, evaporated milk, butter or margarine, and salt. Cook and stir over medium heat about 12 minutes or till mixture is thickened and bubbly. Stir in flaked coconut and pecans; cool. Frosts top of one 13x9-inch cake, tops of two 8- or 9-inch layers, or about 18 cupcakes.

Penuche Frosting

½ **cup butter *or* margarine**
1 **cup packed brown sugar**
¼ **cup milk**
3 **cups sifted powdered sugar**

In medium saucepan melt butter; stir in brown sugar. Cook and stir till bubbly. Remove from heat. Add milk; beat vigorously till smooth. By hand, beat in enough powdered sugar to make of spreading consistency. Quickly frost top of one 13x9-inch cake or tops of two 8- or 9-inch layers.

Powdered Sugar Icing (pictured on pages 22, and 72 and 73; cream cheese variation pictured on the cover)

1 **cup sifted powdered sugar**
¼ **teaspoon vanilla**
Milk

Stir together powdered sugar, vanilla, and enough milk (about 1½ tablespoons) to make of pouring consistency. Glaze or drizzle over top of tube cake, bar cookies, or cookies.

Cream Cheese Icing: Beat together one 3-ounce package softened *cream cheese* and powdered sugar till fluffy. Beat in vanilla. If necessary, beat in enough milk (about 1 teaspoon) to make of pouring consistency. Cover; store in refrigerator.

Chocolate Icing (pictured on pages 18 and 19)

1 **4-ounce package German sweet chocolate, broken up**
3 **tablespoons butter *or* margarine**
1½ **cups sifted powdered sugar**
3 **tablespoons hot water**

In a small saucepan melt German sweet chocolate and butter or margarine over low heat. Remove from heat; stir in powdered sugar and hot water. Add additional hot water, if necessary, to make of pouring consistency. Glaze or drizzle over top of a 10-inch tube cake.

Vanilla Cream Filling (pictured on page 29)

⅓ **cup sugar**
2 **tablespoons all-purpose flour**
1 **tablespoon cornstarch**
¼ **teaspoon salt**
1¼ **cups milk**
1 **tablespoon butter *or* margarine**
2 **slightly beaten eggs**
1 **tablespoon brandy *or* desired liqueur (optional)**
1 **teaspoon vanilla**

In a saucepan thoroughly combine sugar, flour, cornstarch, and salt. Stir in milk; add butter or margarine. Cook and stir over medium heat till thickened and bubbly. Reduce heat; cook and stir 2 minutes more. Gradually stir about half of the hot mixture into eggs; return to remaining hot mixture. Cook and stir till nearly bubbly; reduce heat. Cook and stir 1 to 2 minutes more but *do not boil*.

Remove from heat; stir in brandy and vanilla. Cover surface with waxed paper; cool without stirring, then chill. Makes enough filling to spread between 3 cake layers.

Fig Filling (pictured on pages 18 and 19)

1 **cup finely chopped dried figs (6 ounces)**
1 **cup water**
⅓ **cup light corn syrup**
⅓ **cup sugar**
¼ **cup all-purpose flour**
Dash salt
1 **tablespoon lemon juice**

In a 1½-quart saucepan combine figs and water. Cover and simmer for 20 minutes. Remove from heat; stir in corn syrup. In a mixing bowl combine sugar, flour, and salt; stir into fig mixture. Cook and stir till thickened and bubbly. Remove from heat; stir in lemon juice. Cool. Makes enough filling to spread between 3 or 4 cake layers.

Date Filling: Prepare Fig Filling as above *except* substitute 1 cup finely snipped pitted whole *dates* for the I cup finely chopped dried figs.

Lemon Filling (pictured on pages 18 and 19)

¾ cup sugar
2 tablespoons cornstarch
2 beaten egg yolks
1 teaspoon finely shredded
   lemon peel
3 tablespoons lemon juice
1 tablespoon butter or margarine

In a saucepan combine sugar, cornstarch, and dash *salt*; gradually stir in ¾ cup cold *water*. Add beaten egg yolks, lemon peel, and lemon juice. Cook and stir till mixture is thickened and bubbly. Cook 1 to 2 minutes more; remove from heat. Stir in butter or margarine. Cover surface with waxed paper; cool without stirring. Makes enough filling to spread between 2 cake layers.

Strawberry Sauce (pictured on page 15)

4 cups fresh or frozen
   unsweetened strawberries
1 cup water
¾ cup sugar
2 tablespoons cornstarch
   Few drops red food coloring
   (optional)

Thaw strawberries, if frozen; drain. In a saucepan crush *1 cup* of the strawberries; add water. Cook for 2 minutes; sieve. Combine sugar and cornstarch; stir into sieved mixture. Cook and stir till thickened and bubbly. Cook 1 to 2 minutes more. Add food coloring, if desired. Halve remaining large berries. Stir remaining berries into sauce; chill. Serve over cake. Makes about 3½ cups sauce.

Cinnamon Blueberry Sauce

½ cup sugar
4 teaspoons cornstarch
½ teaspoon finely shredded
   lemon peel
¼ teaspoon ground cinnamon
   Dash salt
1½ cups fresh or frozen
   unsweetened blueberries
1 teaspoon lemon juice

In a small bowl stir together sugar, cornstarch, lemon peel, cinnamon, and salt; set aside. In a saucepan combine ½ *cup* of the blueberries and ⅔ cup *water*. Bring to boiling; remove from heat. Mash berries. Stir in sugar mixture.

Cook and stir over medium heat till mixture is thickened and bubbly. Stir in remaining blueberries and lemon juice; simmer for 3 to 5 minutes or till heated through. Serve over cake. Makes about 1¾ cups sauce.

Cherry Sauce (pictured on pages 18 and 19)

1 16-ounce can pitted dark
   sweet cherries
2 tablespoons cornstarch
2 tablespoons sugar

Drain cherries, reserving syrup. Halve cherries; set aside. Add enough water to the reserved syrup to make 1⅔ cups liquid. In a small saucepan combine cornstarch and sugar; gradually stir in the 1⅔ cups cherry liquid. Cook and stir till thickened and bubbly. Stir in cherries. Cool slightly. Serve over cake. Makes about 2½ cups sauce.

Caramel Pecan Sauce

½ cup packed brown sugar
1 tablespoon cornstarch
¼ teaspoon salt
⅓ cup light cream
2 tablespoons light corn syrup
¼ cup coarsely chopped pecans
1 tablespoon butter or margarine
1 tablespoon rum or brandy

In a heavy saucepan combine brown sugar, cornstarch, and salt. Stir in ¼ cup *water*. Stir in light cream and corn syrup. Cook, stirring constantly, till thickened and bubbly (mixture may appear curdled during cooking). Stir in the coarsely chopped pecans, the butter or margarine, and rum or brandy. Remove from heat. Cover; cool to room temperature. Serve over cake. Makes about 1 cup sauce.

Decorating Cakes & Cookies

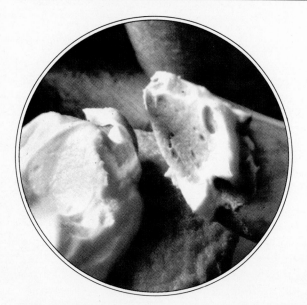

You can use frostings and trimmings to decorate both cakes and cookies. For easy dessert dress-ups, create a design with contrasting icing or etch a pattern in the frosting. Trimming with a topping—such as toasted coconut, nuts, chocolate curls, colored·sugar, or candies—is a quick way to add color and texture. The following suggestions will show you how to use simple decorations to make your cakes and cookies more appealing.

Shadow icing (sometimes called allegretti frosting) is an easy trim for frosted or unfrosted cakes. To make shadow icing, in a saucepan combine 1 square (1 ounce) unsweetened chocolate and ½ teaspoon shortening. Heat and stir over low heat till melted. Drizzle from tip of a teaspoon around edge of cake so chocolate will run down sides.

To create a web pattern, drizzle shadow icing (above) or Powdered Sugar Icing (see recipe, page 52) in circles around top of frosted tube cake. Draw a knife through icing from center to outside edge at regular intervals. Or, drizzle in parallel lines across a frosted round, square, or oblong cake or bar cookies. Draw a knife diagonally through the icing.

To make chocolate curls, use a bar of sweet chocolate at room temperature. Shave thin slices from the flat surface of the chocolate bar with a vegetable peeler. The chocolate will curl as you cut the slice.

For grated chocolate, rub chocolate across rough surface of small-sized hand grater to obtain small, fine pieces.

To create scalloped finish in firm frosting, press tip of spoon in rows on top of a cake or bar cookies. Make rows around a round cake or across an oblong or a square cake or across bar cookies. To prevent the frosting from sticking to the spoon, dip the tip of the spoon in warm water between impressions.

Make a crisscross pattern in firm frosting to trim a cake or bar cookies. Simply draw the tines of a fork through the frosting on top of the cake or bar cookies, forming evenly spaced rows of parallel lines. At right angles to the first rows, draw the fork through the frosting again, making evenly spaced rows.

For a spiral finish, draw a small metal spatula or a knife in a spiral shape through firm frosting on top of a round cake. Work from the center top to the outside edge. Smooth any rough areas by dipping the spatula in warm water and then retouching the desired area. You can form a small spiral on frosted cupcakes or cookies.

Trim an unfrosted dark-colored cake or bar cookies with a powdered sugar design. Position a paper doily on top of the cake or bar cookies. Sift powdered sugar over the doily through a tea strainer, tapping the strainer with your fingers. Gently press the sugar through doily with the back of a spoon, then carefully lift off doily.

Dress up a frosted cake or cookie by sprinkling it with a colorful and flavorful topping. You can use coconut (plain, toasted, or tinted), nuts, fresh or candied fruits and peels, chocolate shot, colored sugar, or small candies. Add these trims to the entire surface or form a border or a design.

For sandwich cookies, spread desired filling or frosting, or peanut butter and jelly over the bottoms of half of the baked cookies. Position the remaining cookies on top of the filling. Also, try placing milk chocolate squares between warm cookies; the chocolate will melt as the cookies cool.

Quick&Easy Cookies

Cheesecake Cookies, Santa's Whiskers, Double Peanut Butter Cookies, Orange Drop Cookies, Pumpkin Drop Cookies, and Chocolate Chip Bars (See Index for recipe pages.)

Drop Cookies

Drop cookies are fast cookie-jar fillers because they are easy to prepare. Their familiar shape is formed by dropping the stiff dough from a spoon onto a cookie sheet. Add nuts, fruits, or cereals to give them texture and flavor.

*I*n cookie making, creaming the butter, margarine, or shortening and the sugar is an important step. If done by hand, first let butter, margarine, or shortening stand at room temperature till softened. In a bowl cream together butter and sugar using the back of a wooden spoon to rub mixture against side of bowl. If using an electric mixer, in a mixer bowl beat butter, margarine, or shortening for 30 seconds, then add sugar (you can omit the softening step). Continue creaming the mixture by hand or mixer until it is well blended and creamy, as shown.

*A*fter preparing the cookie dough, drop it from a teaspoon onto a cookie sheet. Use a spatula to push dough off spoon. Drop dough about 2 inches apart to allow for spreading. Avoid excessive spreading by baking all cookies on cool cookie sheets. To test for doneness, gently touch the lightly browned cookie with fingertip; the imprint should be barely visible. Underbaked cookies are doughy; overbaked cookies are dry and hard. When cookies test done, remove them from cookie sheet using a pancake turner or wide metal spatula. Cool cookies on wire rack before stacking.

Chocolate Chip Cookies (pictured on page 61)

2½ cups all-purpose flour
1 teaspoon baking soda
½ teaspoon salt
½ cup butter *or* margarine
½ cup shortening
1 cup packed brown sugar
½ cup sugar
2 eggs
1½ teaspoons vanilla
1 12-ounce package (2 cups) semisweet chocolate pieces
1 cup chopped walnuts *or* pecans

Stir together flour, baking soda, and salt. In mixer bowl beat butter or margarine and shortening on medium speed of electric mixer for 30 seconds. Add brown sugar and sugar and beat till fluffy. Add eggs and vanilla; beat well.

Add dry ingredients to beaten mixture and beat till well blended. Stir in chocolate pieces and nuts. Drop dough from a teaspoon 2 inches apart onto an ungreased cookie sheet. Bake in 375° oven for 8 to 10 minutes or till done. Remove from cookie sheet; cool on wire rack. Makes about 72.

Double Chocolate Drops (pictured on pages 72 and 73)

1½ **cups all-purpose flour**
½ **teaspoon baking powder**
½ **teaspoon baking soda**
¼ **teaspoon salt**
½ **cup shortening**
2 **squares (2 ounces)**
    unsweetened chocolate
1 **cup packed brown sugar**
1 **egg**
½ **cup buttermilk *or* sour milk**
1 **teaspoon vanilla**
1 **6-ounce package (1 cup)**
    semisweet chocolate pieces
½ **cup chopped walnuts**
    Mocha Butter Frosting
    Toasted coconut (optional)

Stir together flour, baking powder, baking soda, and salt. In medium saucepan melt shortening and unsweetened chocolate over low heat. Cool 10 minutes. Stir in brown sugar. Add egg, buttermilk or sour milk, and vanilla; beat till smooth.

Add dry ingredients to saucepan mixture and beat till well blended. Stir in chocolate pieces and nuts. Drop from a teaspoon 2 inches apart onto a greased cookie sheet. Bake in 350° oven about 10 minutes or till done. Cool about 1 minute before removing to wire rack; cool thoroughly. Frost cookies with Mocha Butter Frosting. Sprinkle with toasted coconut, if desired. Makes about 42.

Mocha Butter Frosting: Beat together ¼ cup *butter or margarine*, 2 tablespoons unsweetened *cocoa powder*, and 2 teaspoons instant *coffee crystals*. Stir in 2½ cups sifted *powdered sugar*, 1½ teaspoons *vanilla*, and enough *milk* (about 2 to 3 tablespoons) to make of spreading consistency.

Oatmeal Chippers (pictured on the cover)

1½ **cups all-purpose flour**
1 **teaspoon baking soda**
½ **cup butter *or* margarine**
½ **cup shortening**
1 **cup sugar**
1 **cup packed brown sugar**
2 **eggs**
1 **teaspoon vanilla**
3 **cups quick-cooking rolled oats**
1 **6-ounce package (1 cup)**
    semisweet chocolate pieces
1 **cup coarsely chopped salted**
    peanuts

Stir together flour and baking soda. In mixer bowl beat butter or margarine and shortening on medium speed of electric mixer for 30 seconds. Add sugar and brown sugar, and beat till fluffy. Add eggs and vanilla; beat well. Add dry ingredients to beaten mixture and beat till well blended. Stir in oats, chocolate pieces, and peanuts. Drop from a teaspoon 2 inches apart onto an ungreased cookie sheet. Bake in 375° oven for 8 to 10 minutes or till done. Remove from cookie sheet; cool on wire rack. Makes about 72.

Storing & Freezing Cookies

Cookie Jar Storage: For short-time storage, place cookies in covered containers with snug-fitting lids. Store soft cookies and crisp cookies in separate containers or the crisp ones will become soft.

If soft cookies begin to dry out, place an apple half, skin side down, on top of the cookies in the storage container. Remove and discard the fruit after a day or two. For ease, store bar cookies in the pan in which they were baked. Cover the baking pan tightly.

Freezing Cookies: For longer storage, freeze baked cookies in freezer containers, freezer bags, or foil for up to 12 months. (Pack fragile cookies in freezer containers.) Before serving, thaw cookies in freezer wrappings.

To freeze unbaked cookies, pack dough into freezer containers or shape stiff dough into rolls and wrap securely in foil. Freeze up to 6 months.

Lacy Oatmeal Crisps (pictured on page 61)

2 cups quick-cooking rolled oats
½ teaspoon baking soda
¼ teaspoon salt
1 cup packed brown sugar
½ cup shortening
¼ cup butter *or* margarine
1 beaten egg

Stir together oats, baking soda, and salt. In large saucepan combine brown sugar, shortening, and butter or margarine. Cook and stir over low heat till melted; remove from heat. Stir in dry ingredients. Add egg; mix well.

Drop from a teaspoon 3 inches apart onto greased cookie sheet; stir remaining batter often. Bake in 375° oven for 6 to 7 minutes or till done. Cool about 2 minutes before removing to wire rack; cool. Makes about 48.

Two-Tone Cookies

1¾ cups all-purpose flour
½ teaspoon baking soda
½ teaspoon salt
½ cup butter *or* margarine
½ cup sugar
½ cup packed brown sugar
1 egg
1 teaspoon vanilla
¾ cup dairy sour cream
¼ cup chopped walnuts
1 square (1 ounce) unsweetened
    chocolate, melted and cooled
Walnut halves

Stir together flour, baking soda, and salt. In mixer bowl beat butter or margarine on medium speed of electric mixer for 30 seconds. Add sugar and brown sugar, and beat till fluffy. Add egg and vanilla; beat well. Stir in sour cream. Add dry ingredients to beaten mixture and beat till well combined. Stir in ¼ cup chopped walnuts.

Divide dough in half. Stir melted chocolate into one half. Drop from a teaspoon 2 inches apart onto an ungreased cookie sheet. Using the remaining plain dough, drop from a teaspoon next to each chocolate mound. (The mounds of dough will bake together.) Lightly press a walnut half onto each cookie. Bake in 375° oven for 12 to 15 minutes or till done. Remove from cookie sheet; cool on rack. Makes about 24.

Giant Peanut Butter-Apple Cookies

1 cup all-purpose flour
1 cup whole wheat flour
2 teaspoons baking soda
¾ teaspoon salt
¾ cup peanut butter
¼ cup butter *or* margarine
2 cups packed brown sugar
2 eggs
1 teaspoon vanilla
1 cup quick-cooking rolled oats
1 cup chopped peeled apple

Stir together all-purpose flour, whole wheat flour, baking soda, and salt. In mixer bowl beat peanut butter and butter or margarine on medium speed of electric mixer for 30 seconds. Add brown sugar and beat till fluffy. Add eggs and vanilla; beat well. Add dry ingredients to beaten mixture and beat till well blended. Stir in the oats and apple.

For each cookie, spoon about l/4 cup dough onto ungreased cookie sheet; flatten slightly with fingers. Bake in 350° oven for l2 to l4 minutes or till done. Cool about 1 minute before removing to wire rack; cool. Makes about 20.

No-Bake Drop Cookies

2 cups sugar
¼ cup unsweetened cocoa
    powder
½ cup milk
½ cup butter *or* margarine
1 tablespoon light corn syrup
¼ cup peanut butter
2 cups quick-cooking rolled oats

In heavy saucepan stir together sugar and cocoa powder; stir in milk. Add butter or margarine and corn syrup; bring to boiling, stirring occasionally. Boil vigorously for 3 minutes. Stir in peanut butter, then rolled oats.

Return mixture to boiling. Remove from heat; beat till slightly thickened. Immediately drop from a teaspoon onto waxed paper. (If mixture spreads too much, beat a little longer.) Cool. Makes about 36.

Pecan Crispies

1¼ cups all-purpose flour
1 teaspoon baking powder
¼ teaspoon baking soda
¼ teaspoon salt
½ cup butter *or* margarine
⅓ cup sugar
⅓ cup packed brown sugar
1 egg
½ teaspoon vanilla
1 cup chopped pecans

Stir together flour, baking powder, baking soda, and salt. In mixer bowl beat butter or margarine on medium speed of electric mixer for 30 seconds. Add sugar and brown sugar, and beat till fluffy. Add egg and vanilla; beat well.

Add dry ingredients to beaten mixture and beat till well blended. Stir in pecans. Drop from a teaspoon 2 inches apart onto an ungreased cookie sheet. Bake in 375° oven for 8 to 10 minutes or till done. Cool about 1 minute before removing to wire rack; cool. Makes about 30.

Cocoa Drop Cookies

2½ cups all-purpose flour
½ cup unsweetened cocoa powder
1 teaspoon baking powder
1 teaspoon baking soda
½ teaspoon salt
1 cup butter *or* margarine
1¾ cups sugar
1 cup cream-style cottage cheese
2 eggs
1 teaspoon vanilla

Stir together flour, cocoa powder, baking powder, baking soda, and salt. In mixer bowl beat butter or margarine on medium speed of electric mixer for 30 seconds. Add sugar and cottage cheese; beat till fluffy and smooth. Add eggs and vanilla; beat well. Add dry ingredients to beaten mixture and beat till well blended.

Drop from a teaspoon 2 inches apart onto an ungreased cookie sheet. Bake in 350° oven for 10 to 12 minutes or till done. Cool about 1 minute before removing to wire rack; cool. Frost as desired. Makes about 72.

Lemon Tea Cookies

2 teaspoons lemon juice
½ cup milk
1¾ cups all-purpose flour
1 teaspoon baking powder
¼ teaspoon baking soda
½ cup butter *or* margarine
¾ cup sugar
1 egg
1 teaspoon grated lemon peel
¾ cup sugar
¼ cup lemon juice

Stir 2 teaspoons lemon juice into milk; set aside. Stir together flour, baking powder, baking soda, and ¼ teaspoon *salt*. In mixer bowl beat butter for 30 seconds. Add ¾ cup sugar; beat till fluffy. Add egg and lemon peel; beat well.

Add dry ingredients and milk mixture alternately to beaten mixture and beat till well blended. Drop from a teaspoon 2 inches apart onto an ungreased cookie sheet. Bake in 350° oven for 12 to 14 minutes or till done. Combine ¾ cup sugar and lemon juice; stir till sugar is dissolved. Remove cookies at once to a wire rack; brush with lemon mixture. Cool. Makes about 48.

Jam-Topped Drop Cookies

2¼ cups all-purpose flour
2 teaspoons baking powder
½ teaspoon salt
¾ cup butter *or* margarine
⅔ cup sugar
1 egg
¼ cup pineapple *or* cherry preserves
¼ cup milk
Pineapple *or* cherry preserves
Blanched almond halves

Stir together flour, baking powder, and salt. In mixer bowl beat butter or margarine on medium speed of electric mixer for 30 seconds. Add sugar and beat till fluffy. Add egg, ¼ cup preserves, and milk; beat well. Add dry ingredients to beaten mixture and beat till well blended.

Drop from teaspoon 2 inches apart onto an ungreased cookie sheet. Bake in 375° oven for 8 to 10 minutes or till done. Cool about 1 minute before removing to wire rack; cool. Spoon about ½ teaspoon additional preserves onto each cookie; top with a blanched almond half. Makes about 48.

Bake a batch of these drop cookie favorites: *Jam-Topped Drop Cookies,*
Chocolate Chip Cookies (see recipe, page 57), or *Lacy Oatmeal Crisps* (see recipe, page 59).

Pumpkin Drop Cookies (pictured on page 56)

2 cups all-purpose flour
1 teaspoon baking powder
1 teaspoon ground cinnamon
½ teaspoon baking soda
½ teaspoon ground nutmeg
½ cup butter *or* margarine
1 cup packed brown sugar
1 egg
1 cup canned pumpkin
1 teaspoon vanilla
1 cup raisins
½ cup chopped walnuts

Stir together flour, baking powder, cinnamon, baking soda, and nutmeg. In mixer bowl beat butter or margarine on medium speed of electric mixer for 30 seconds. Add brown sugar and beat till fluffy. Add egg, canned pumpkin, and vanilla; beat well.

Add dry ingredients to beaten mixture and beat till well blended. Stir in raisins and walnuts. (Dough will be soft.) Drop from a teaspoon 2 inches apart onto a greased cookie sheet. Bake in 375° oven for 8 to 10 minutes or till done. Remove from cookie sheet; cool on wire rack. Makes about 48.

Banana Drop Cookies

2 cups all-purpose flour
1½ teaspoons baking powder
½ teaspoon ground cinnamon
¼ teaspoon baking soda
¼ teaspoon salt
¼ teaspoon ground cloves
½ cup butter *or* margarine
1 cup sugar
2 eggs
½ teaspoon vanilla
2 medium bananas, mashed
   (1 cup)
½ cup chopped walnuts
Banana Butter Frosting

Stir together flour, baking powder, cinnamon, baking soda, salt, and cloves. In mixer bowl beat butter or margarine on medium speed of electric mixer for 30 seconds. Add sugar and beat till fluffy. Add eggs and vanilla; beat well. Add dry ingredients and banana alternately to beaten mixture and beat till well blended. Stir in walnuts.

Drop from a teaspoon 2 inches apart onto a greased cookie sheet. Bake in 375° oven for 10 to 12 minutes or till done. Immediately remove from cookie sheet; cool on wire rack. Frost with Banana Butter Frosting. Makes about 60.

Banana Butter Frosting: Beat together 2 cups sifted *powdered sugar,* ¼ cup mashed *banana,* 2 tablespoons softened *butter,* and ½ teaspoon *vanilla.* If necessary, beat in additional powdered sugar to make of spreading consistency.

Orange Drop Cookies (pictured on pages 56 and 81)

3½ cups all-purpose flour
2 teaspoons baking powder
1 teaspoon baking soda
¾ cup shortening
¼ cup butter *or* margarine
1½ cups packed brown sugar
2 eggs
2 tablespoons grated orange peel
¼ cup orange juice
1 teaspoon vanilla
1 cup buttermilk *or* sour milk
1 cup chopped nuts

Stir together flour, baking powder, baking soda, and ¼ teaspoon *salt.* In mixer bowl beat shortening and butter or margarine on medium speed of electric mixer for 30 seconds. Add brown sugar and beat till fluffy. Add eggs, orange peel, orange juice, and vanilla; beat well. Add dry ingredients and buttermilk or sour milk alternately to beaten mixture and beat till well blended. Stir in nuts.

Drop from a teaspoon 2 inches apart onto a greased cookie sheet. Bake in 350° oven for 12 to 15 minutes. Cool about 1 minute; remove to wire rack. Cool. If desired, frost cookies with Orange Butter Frosting (see recipe, page 50) and sprinkle with additional grated orange peel. Makes about 72.

Coconut Macaroons (pictured on pages 4 and 5)

2 egg whites
½ teaspoon vanilla
⅔ cup sugar
1 3½-ounce can flaked coconut

Beat egg whites, vanilla, and dash *salt* till soft peaks form. Gradually add sugar, beating to stiff peaks. Fold in coconut. Drop from a teaspoon onto greased cookie sheet. Bake in 325° oven about 20 minutes; cool. Makes 20 to 24.

Hermits (pictured on pages 4 and 5)

1½ cups all-purpose flour
½ teaspoon baking soda
½ teaspoon ground cinnamon
¼ teaspoon ground nutmeg
¼ teaspoon ground cloves
½ cup butter *or* margarine
¾ cup packed brown sugar
1 egg
2 tablespoons milk
1 teaspoon vanilla
1 cup raisins
½ cup chopped walnuts

Stir together flour, baking soda, cinnamon, nutmeg, cloves, and ¼ teaspoon *salt*. In mixer bowl beat butter or margarine on medium speed of electric mixer for 30 seconds. Add brown sugar and beat till fluffy. Add egg, milk, and vanilla; beat well. Add dry ingredients to beaten mixture and beat till well blended. Stir in raisins and walnuts.

Drop dough from a teaspoon 2 inches apart onto a greased cookie sheet. Bake in 375° oven for 10 to 12 minutes or till done. Remove from cookie sheet; cool on wire rack. Makes about 36.

Ranger Cookies

1¼ cups all-purpose flour
½ teaspoon baking powder
½ teaspoon baking soda
½ cup butter *or* margarine
½ cup sugar
½ cup packed brown sugar
1 egg
1 teaspoon vanilla
2 cups crisp rice cereal
1 3½-ounce can flaked coconut
1 cup pitted whole dates, snipped, *or* raisins

Stir together flour, baking powder, baking soda, and ¼ teaspoon *salt*. In mixer bowl beat butter or margarine on medium speed of electric mixer for 30 seconds. Add sugar and brown sugar and beat till fluffy. Add egg and vanilla; beat well.

Add dry ingredients to beaten mixture and beat till well blended. Stir in cereal, coconut, and dates or raisins. Drop from a teaspoon 2 inches apart onto an ungreased cookie sheet. Bake in 375° oven for 8 to 10 minutes or till done. Cool about 1 minute before removing to wire rack; cool. Makes about 48.

Bran Puff Cookies

1¾ cups all-purpose flour
½ teaspoon baking soda
½ cup butter *or* margarine
½ cup sugar
½ cup packed brown sugar
1 egg
½ cup dairy sour cream
1 teaspoon vanilla
1 cup 40 percent bran flakes
½ cup raisins

Stir together flour, baking soda, and ½ teaspoon *salt*. In mixer bowl beat butter or margarine on medium speed of electric mixer for 30 seconds. Add sugar and brown sugar and beat till fluffy. Add egg, sour cream, and vanilla; beat well. Add dry ingredients to beaten mixture and beat till well blended. Stir in cereal and raisins. Drop from a teaspoon 2 inches apart onto a greased cookie sheet. Bake in 375° oven for 10 to 12 minutes or till done. Remove from cookie sheet; cool on wire rack. Makes about 48.

Mincemeat Cookies

3 cups all-purpose flour
1 teaspoon baking soda
¼ teaspoon salt
1 cup butter *or* margarine
1½ cups sugar
3 eggs
1¾ cups prepared mincemeat
½ cup chopped walnuts

Stir together flour, baking soda, and salt. In mixer bowl beat butter or margarine on medium speed of electric mixer for 30 seconds. Add sugar, and beat till fluffy. Add eggs; beat well. Add dry ingredients to beaten mixture and beat till well blended. Stir in mincemeat and nuts.

Drop dough from a teaspoon 2 inches apart onto a greased cookie sheet. Bake in 350° oven for 12 to 14 minutes or till done. Remove to wire rack; cool. Makes about 72.

Wheat Germ-Molasses Date Cookies

2 cups all-purpose flour
⅓ cup wheat germ
1 teaspoon salt
1 teaspoon ground cinnamon
½ teaspoon baking powder
½ teaspoon baking soda
1 8-ounce package (1½ cups) pitted whole dates, snipped
½ cup molasses
½ cup honey
2 tablespoons water
½ cup cooking oil
2 eggs
1 teaspoon finely shredded orange peel
1 teaspoon vanilla
⅓ cup shelled sunflower seed

Stir together flour, wheat germ, salt, cinnamon, baking powder, and baking soda. In saucepan combine snipped dates, molasses, honey, and water; simmer for 2 minutes. Remove from heat.

Stir in cooking oil; cool. Beat in eggs, orange peel, and vanilla. Add dry ingredients to date mixture and beat till well blended. Stir in sunflower seed. Drop from a teaspoon 2 inches apart onto a greased cookie sheet. Bake in 375° oven for 7 to 8 minutes or till done. Cool about 1 minute before removing to wire rack; cool. Makes about 72.

Ginger Creams

2 cups all-purpose flour
1 teaspoon ground ginger
½ teaspoon baking soda
½ teaspoon ground cinnamon
½ teaspoon ground nutmeg
¼ teaspoon ground cloves
¼ cup shortening
½ cup sugar
1 egg
½ cup molasses
½ cup water
Lemon Butter Frosting (see recipe, page 50)

Stir together flour, ginger, baking soda, cinnamon, nutmeg, and cloves. In mixer bowl beat shortening on medium speed of electric mixer for 30 seconds. Add sugar and beat till fluffy. Add egg and molasses; beat well. Add dry ingredients and water alternately to beaten mixture and beat till well blended. (Dough will be soft.)

Drop from a teaspoon 2 inches apart onto a greased cookie sheet. Bake in 350° oven for 10 to 12 minutes or till done. Remove from cookie sheet; cool on wire rack. Frost with Lemon Butter Frosting. Makes about 36.

Toffee Drop Cookies

3½ cups all-purpose flour
1 teaspoon baking powder
1 teaspoon baking soda
1 teaspoon salt
1 cup butter *or* margarine
1½ cups packed brown sugar
2 eggs
¼ cup milk
2 teaspoons vanilla
6 1¹/₁₆-ounce bars chocolate-coated English toffee, chilled and crushed (about 1¼ cups)

Stir together flour, baking powder, baking soda, and salt. In mixer bowl beat butter or margarine on medium speed of electric mixer for 30 seconds. Add brown sugar and beat till fluffy. Add eggs, milk, and vanilla; beat well.

Add dry ingredients to beaten mixture and beat till well blended. Stir in crushed candy. Drop from a teaspoon 2 inches apart onto an ungreased cookie sheet. Bake in 375° oven about 10 minutes or till done. Remove from cookie sheet; cool on wire rack. Makes about 60.

Sliced Cookies

Prepare now; bake later. Sliced cookies are easy to prepare and can wait until you're ready to bake them. Just shape the dough into a roll, refrigerate until firm, and cut into slices. Chill any remaining dough for use later in the week.

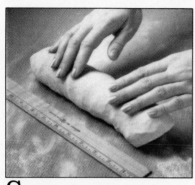

*S*hape prepared cookie dough into a roll by working it with your hands and rolling it on the counter until it measures the desired length, as shown.

You can dress up basic dough by rolling the shaped roll in finely chopped nuts or flaked coconut. Gently press roll into the coating so it will stick.

*W*rap the roll in clear plastic wrap or waxed paper. Chill dough several hours or overnight. You can store the tightly wrapped dough in the refrigerator for up to 1 week, or in the freezer for up to 6 months.

*I*f necessary, reshape roll slightly to round out flattened side. Cut dough into slices using a sharp, thin-bladed knife. If dough softens during slicing, place it in the freezer till firm enough to slice neatly. Again, reshape each slice as needed to round out the flattened side of the roll.

Refrigerator Cookies

2¼ cups all-purpose flour
  1 teaspoon ground cinnamon
  ½ teaspoon baking soda
  ½ teaspoon salt
  ¼ teaspoon ground nutmeg
  ¼ teaspoon ground cloves
  ½ cup butter *or* margarine
  ½ cup shortening
  ½ cup sugar
  ½ cup packed brown sugar
  1 egg
  2 tablespoons milk
  ½ teaspoon vanilla
  ½ cup finely chopped nuts

Stir together flour, cinnamon, baking soda, salt, nutmeg, and cloves. In mixer bowl beat butter or margarine and shortening on medium speed of electric mixer for 30 seconds. Add sugar and brown sugar and beat till fluffy. Add egg, milk, and vanilla; beat well. Add dry ingredients to beaten mixture and beat till well blended. Stir in nuts. Cover and chill about 45 minutes for easier handling. Shape into two 7-inch-long rolls. Wrap in waxed paper or clear plastic wrap; chill at least 6 hours or overnight.

Cut dough into ¼-inch slices. Place 1 inch apart on a greased cookie sheet. Bake in 375° oven for 8 to 10 minutes or till done. Cool about 1 minute before removing to wire rack; cool. Makes about 60.

Whole Wheat Refrigerator Cookies: Prepare Refrigerator Cookies as above *except* use only *1½ cups* all-purpose flour and add 1 cup *whole wheat flour*. Roll shaped dough in ¼ cup *wheat germ* to coat surface before second chilling.

Oatmeal Refrigerator Cookies

1½ **cups all-purpose flour**
1 **teaspoon baking soda**
1 **teaspoon ground cinnamon**
⅛ **teaspoon ground cloves**
½ **cup shortening**
½ **cup butter *or* margarine**
1 **cup packed brown sugar**
2 **eggs**
1 **teaspoon vanilla**
1½ **cups quick-cooking rolled oats**

Stir together flour, baking soda, cinnamon, cloves, and 1 teaspoon *salt*. Beat shortening and butter with electric mixer for 30 seconds. Add brown sugar and beat till fluffy. Add eggs and vanilla; beat well. Add dry ingredients to beaten mixture and beat till well blended. Stir in oats. Stir in ½ cup finely chopped *nuts*, if desired. Shape dough into two 8-inch-long rolls. Wrap in waxed paper or clear plastic wrap; chill thoroughly. Cut into ¼-inch slices. Place on a greased cookie sheet. Bake in 375° oven for 8 to 10 minutes or till done. Remove to wire rack; cool. Makes about 60.

Double Peanut Butter Cookies (also pictured on page 56)

1½ **cups all-purpose flour**
½ **teaspoon baking soda**
¼ **teaspoon salt**
½ **cup butter *or* margarine**
½ **cup peanut butter**
⅓ **cup sugar**
⅓ **cup packed brown sugar**
3 **tablespoons orange juice**
Peanut Butter

Combine flour, soda, and salt. Beat butter and ½ cup peanut butter for 30 seconds. Add sugar and brown sugar; beat till fluffy. Add dry ingredients and orange juice; beat well. Shape into 7-inch-long roll. Wrap in waxed paper; chill thoroughly. Cut into ⅛-to ¼-inch slices.

Place half the slices on ungreased cookie sheet. Spread each center with about 1 teaspoon peanut butter. Cover with remaining slices. Let stand till slightly softened; seal edges with fork. Bake in 350° oven for 12 to 15 minutes or till done. Cool 1 minute; remove. Cool. Makes 18 to 24.

Sugar Pecan Crisps

1¾ **cups all-purpose flour**
¼ **teaspoon salt**
¾ **cup butter *or* margarine**
⅔ **cup sugar**
1 **egg**
1 **teaspoon vanilla**
½ **cup finely chopped pecans**

Combine flour and salt. Beat butter for 30 seconds. Add sugar; beat till fluffy. Add egg and vanilla; beat well. Add dry ingredients; beat till well blended. Cover; chill 30 to 60 minutes for easier handling. Shape into a 12-inch-long roll. Roll in nuts. Wrap in waxed paper; chill several hours or overnight. Cut into ¼-inch slices. Place on ungreased cookie sheet. Bake in 350° oven for 10 to 12 minutes or till done. Remove to wire rack; cool. Makes about 48.

Chocolate Coconut Slices

1 **3-ounce package cream cheese, softened**
⅓ **cup sugar**
2 **teaspoons vanilla**
1 **cup flaked coconut**
½ **cup finely chopped nuts**
1½ **cups all-purpose flour**
½ **teaspoon baking soda**
6 **tablespoons butter**
1 **cup sifted powdered sugar**
1 **egg**
2 **squares (2 ounces) unsweetened chocolate, melted and cooled**

For filling beat cream cheese, sugar, and 1 *teaspoon* vanilla till smooth. Stir in coconut and nuts. Cover; chill. Combine flour, soda, and ½ teaspoon *salt*. Beat butter for 30 seconds. Add powdered sugar; beat till well blended. Add egg, chocolate, and remaining vanilla; beat well. Add dry ingredients; beat till well blended. Cover and chill about 30 minutes. Between 2 pieces of waxed paper, roll dough into a 14x4½-inch rectangle. Remove top paper.

Shape filling into a 14-inch-long roll; place on dough. Roll dough around filling, removing paper; seal edge. Wrap in waxed paper; chill several hours or overnight. Cut into ¼-inch slices. Place on greased cookie sheet. Bake in 375° oven for 8 to 10 minutes or till done. Cool about 1 minute; remove to wire rack. Cool. Makes about 48.

Enjoy *Chocolate Coconut Slices, Date Pinwheels* (see recipe, page 68), *Sugar Pecan Crisps, Orange Refrigerator Cookies* (see recipe, page 68), and *Double Peanut Butter Cookies.*

Date Pinwheels (pictured on page 67)

1 8-ounce package pitted whole dates, finely snipped
⅓ cup sugar
½ cup finely chopped nuts
½ teaspoon vanilla
2⅓ cups all-purpose flour
½ teaspoon baking powder
¼ teaspoon baking soda
¼ teaspoon salt
¼ teaspoon ground cinnamon
½ cup shortening
1 cup packed brown sugar
2 eggs
½ teaspoon vanilla

For filling combine dates, sugar, and ⅓ cup *water*; bring to boiling. Cook and stir over low heat till thickened. Remove from heat; stir in nuts and ½ teaspoon vanilla. Cover; chill. Combine flour, baking powder, soda, salt, and cinnamon. Beat shortening for 30 seconds. Add brown sugar; beat till fluffy. Add eggs and ½ teaspoon vanilla; beat well. Add dry ingredients; beat well. Cover; chill 30 minutes. On waxed paper, roll dough to 18x10-inch rectangle.

Spread filling to within ½ inch of edges. Roll up jelly-roll style, beginning at long side; seal edge. Cut in half crosswise. Wrap rolls; chill several hours or overnight. Cut into ¼-inch slices; place on greased cookie sheet. Bake in 350° oven for 8 to 10 minutes or till done. Cool 1 minute; remove to wire rack. Cool. Makes about 72.

Santa's Whiskers (pictured on page 56)

1 cup butter *or* margarine
1 cup sugar
2 tablespoons milk
1 teaspoon vanilla
2½ cups all-purpose flour
1 cup finely chopped red *or* green candied cherries
½ cup finely chopped pecans
1 cup flaked coconut

Beat butter for 30 seconds. Add sugar; beat till fluffy. Add milk and vanilla; beat well. Stir in flour, then cherries and pecans. Shape into three 7-inch-long rolls. Roll in flaked coconut to coat. (Or, if desired, stir coconut into the dough instead of coating rolls.)

Wrap in waxed paper or clear plastic wrap; chill thoroughly. Cut into ¼-inch slices. Place on ungreased cookie sheet. Bake in 375° oven about 12 minutes or till edges are golden. Remove to wire rack; cool. Makes about 80.

Orange Refrigerator Cookies (pictured on page 67)

3 cups all-purpose flour
¼ teaspoon baking soda
1 cup butter *or* margarine
½ cup sugar
½ cup packed brown sugar
1 egg
1 tablespoon grated orange peel
2 tablespoons orange juice
1 teaspoon vanilla
½ cup finely chopped walnuts

Stir together flour, soda, and ½ teaspoon *salt*. Beat butter for 30 seconds. Add sugars; beat till fluffy. Add egg, orange peel, orange juice, and vanilla; beat well. Add dry ingredients; beat well. Stir in walnuts. Shape into two 8-inch-long rolls. Wrap in clear plastic wrap; chill several hours or overnight. Cut into ¼-inch slices; place on ungreased cookie sheet. Bake in 375° oven for 10 to 12 minutes or till done. Cool about 1 minute before removing to wire rack; cool. If desired, frost with Powdered Sugar Icing (see recipe, page 52). Makes about 64.

Easy Slicing Tip

To make round sliced cookies the easy way, pack dough into clean 6-ounce frozen juice cans (opened at one end only) till it is level with the open top. Cover open end with foil; chill till firm. To slice cookies for baking, open the sealed can end leaving loosened can end against dough; remove foil. Press on can end to push dough out ¼ inch. With a sharp knife, slice even with can end. (Some doughs need to stand at room temperature for 5 to 10 minutes before slicing.)

Bar Cookies

Making bar cookies is as easy as spreading the batter in the pan, baking, and cutting into individual cookies. Some bars are layered with ingredients for a striped effect. Bar cookies can be frosted, dusted with powdered sugar, or served plain.

Spread the batter evenly in the baking pan. For this type of cookie, it is important to use the correct pan size. If you bake bar cookies in a pan that is too large, the cookies will be dry. If the pan is too small, the bars will be underbaked.

Test cake-like bars for doneness with a wooden pick. Fudge-like bars are done when a slight imprint remains after touching lightly.

For a special effect, cut bar cookies into diamond shapes instead of rectangles or squares. Cool bar cookies on a wire rack. With a knife make straight cuts in one direction, and diagonal cuts in the other direction, as shown. The yield for diamond-shaped bars will be slightly fewer than for rectangular or square bar cookies.

Fudge Brownies

½ cup butter *or* margarine
2 squares unsweetened chocolate
1 cup sugar
2 eggs
1 teaspoon vanilla
¾ cup all-purpose flour

Grease an 8x8x2-inch baking pan. Melt together butter and chocolate. Remove from heat; stir in sugar. Add eggs and vanilla; beat lightly just till blended (don't overbeat because brownies will rise too high, then fall). Stir in flour. Stir in ½ cup chopped *nuts*, if desired. Spread in pan. Bake in 350° oven about 30 minutes. Cool. Cut into bars. Makes 16.

Chocolate Syrup Brownies

½ cup butter *or* margarine
1 cup sugar
4 eggs
1 16-ounce can (1½ cups)
    chocolate-flavored syrup
1¼ cups all-purpose flour

Grease a 13x9x2-inch baking pan. Beat butter for 30 seconds. Add sugar and beat till fluffy. Add eggs; beat well. Stir in syrup, then flour. (Batter will look curdled.) Fold in 1 cup chopped *nuts*, if desired. Spread batter in pan. Bake in 350° oven for 30 to 35 minutes or till done. Cool on wire rack. Frost, if desired. Cut into bars. Makes 32.

Chocolate Cream Cheese Brownies

1 **6-ounce package (1 cup) semisweet chocolate pieces**
2 **tablespoons butter**
½ **cup all-purpose flour**
½ **teaspoon baking powder**
2 **eggs**
1 **teaspoon vanilla**
¾ **cup sugar**
½ **cup chopped walnuts**
1 **3-ounce package cream cheese**
¼ **cup sugar**
1 **egg**
½ **teaspoon vanilla**

Grease and lightly flour an 8x8x2-inch baking pan. Melt together chocolate and butter; cool. Stir together flour, baking powder, and ¼ teaspoon *salt*. In mixer bowl beat 2 eggs and 1 teaspoon vanilla with electric mixer; gradually add ¾ cup sugar. Continue beating till thick and lemon-colored. Add dry ingredients to beaten mixture; beat well. Stir in chocolate mixture and nuts; set aside.

Beat cream cheese for 30 seconds. Add ¼ cup sugar; beat till fluffy. Beat in remaining egg and ½ teaspoon vanilla. Spread *half* the chocolate mixture in pan. Pour cheese mixture over; top with remaining chocolate mixture. Swirl layers to marble, if desired. Bake in 350° oven about 45 minutes or till done. Cool. Cut into bars. Makes l6.

Tri-Level Brownies

1 **cup quick-cooking rolled oats**
½ **cup all-purpose flour**
½ **cup packed brown sugar**
¼ **teaspoon baking soda**
6 **tablespoons butter, melted**
¾ **cup sugar**
¼ **cup butter, melted**
1 **square (1 ounce) unsweetened chocolate, melted and cooled**
1 **egg**
½ **teaspoon vanilla**
⅔ **cup all-purpose flour**
¼ **teaspoon baking powder**
¼ **cup milk**
½ **cup chopped walnuts**
1 **square (1 ounce) unsweetened chocolate**
2 **tablespoons butter**
1½ **cups sifted powdered sugar**
1 **teaspoon vanilla**

Stir together oats, the ½ cup flour, the brown sugar, soda, and ¼ teaspoon *salt*. Stir in the 6 tablespoons melted butter. Pat into ungreased 11x7x1½-inch baking pan. Bake in 350° oven for 10 minutes; cool. Combine sugar, the ¼ cup melted butter, and 1 square melted chocolate. Add egg and ½ teaspoon vanilla; beat just till blended. Stir together the ⅔ cup flour, baking powder, and ¼ teaspoon *salt*. Add dry ingredients and milk alternately to chocolate mixture; beat till blended. Stir in chopped nuts. Spread over baked layer. Bake in 350° oven about 25 minutes or till done. Cool.

For frosting, in saucepan melt 1 square chocolate and 2 tablespoons butter over low heat; stir constantly. Remove from heat; stir in powdered sugar and 1 teaspoon vanilla. Stir in enough *hot water* (about 2 tablespoons) to make almost pourable. Frost brownies. If desired, top with walnut halves. Cut into bars. Makes l6.

Chocolate Revel Bars (pictured on pages 72 and 73)

3 **cups quick-cooking rolled oats**
2½ **cups all-purpose flour**
1 **teaspoon baking soda**
1 **cup butter *or* margarine**
2 **cups packed brown sugar**
2 **eggs**
2 **teaspoons vanilla**
1½ **cups semisweet chocolate pieces**
1 **14-ounce can (1¼ cups) *sweetened condensed* milk**
2 **tablespoons butter**
½ **cup chopped walnuts**
2 **teaspoons vanilla**

Stir together oats, flour, baking soda, and 1 teaspoon *salt*. In mixer bowl beat 1 cup butter or margarine on medium speed of electric mixer for 30 seconds. Add brown sugar and beat till fluffy. Add eggs and 2 teaspoons vanilla; beat well. Add dry ingredients to beaten mixture and beat till well blended. In heavy saucepan heat together chocolate pieces, sweetened condensed milk, 2 tablespoons butter, and ½ teaspoon *salt* over low heat, stirring till smooth. Remove from heat. Stir in nuts and 2 teaspoons vanilla.

Pat ⅔ of the oat mixture into bottom of an ungreased 15x10x1-inch baking pan. Spread with chocolate mixture. Dot with remaining oat mixture. Bake in 350° oven 25 to 30 minutes or till done. Cool on wire rack. Cut into bars. Makes 48.

Oatmeal Jam Bars

1⅓ cups all-purpose flour
¼ teaspoon baking soda
¼ teaspoon salt
¾ cup quick-cooking rolled oats
⅓ cup packed brown sugar
1 teaspoon finely shredded
    lemon peel
2 3-ounce packages cream
    cheese
¼ cup butter *or* margarine
¾ cup blackberry *or* peach jam
1 teaspoon lemon juice

Grease a 9x9x2-inch baking pan. Stir together flour, baking soda, and salt. Stir in oats, brown sugar, and lemon peel. In small mixing bowl beat together cream cheese and butter or margarine; cut into dry ingredients till mixture is crumbly and evenly mixed. Set aside 1 cup of the mixture. Pat remaining mixture into bottom of pan. Bake in 350° oven for 20 minutes. Meanwhile, in small bowl combine jam and lemon juice. Spread over baked layer. Sprinkle with the reserved 1 cup mixture. Bake in 350° oven about 15 minutes or till done. Cool on wire rack. Cut into bars. Makes 36.

Apple Butter-Oatmeal Bars

⅔ cup all-purpose flour
½ teaspoon baking powder
½ teaspoon baking soda
¼ teaspoon salt
½ cup butter *or* margarine
½ cup packed brown sugar
1 egg
½ cup apple butter
1 cup quick-cooking rolled oats
1 cup flaked coconut

Grease a 13x9x2-inch baking pan. Stir together flour, baking powder, baking soda, and salt. In mixer bowl beat butter or margarine on medium speed of electric mixer for 30 seconds. Add brown sugar and beat till fluffy. Add egg and apple butter; beat well. Add dry ingredients to beaten mixture and beat till well blended. Stir in oats and coconut. Spread batter in prepared pan.

Bake in 350° oven for 15 to 20 minutes or till done. If desired, sift powdered sugar over top while cookies are warm. Cool on wire rack. Cut into bars. Makes 48.

Peanut Butter Squares (pictured on pages 72 and 73)

1½ cups all-purpose flour
1½ teaspoons baking powder
½ teaspoon salt
½ cup peanut butter
⅓ cup shortening
1½ cups packed brown sugar
2 eggs
1 teaspoon vanilla
¼ cup milk
    Peanut Butter Frosting (see
    recipe, page 50)
⅓ cup chopped peanuts

Grease a 15x10x1-inch baking pan. Stir together flour, baking powder, and salt. In mixer bowl beat peanut butter and shortening on medium speed of electric mixer for 30 seconds. Add brown sugar and beat till fluffy. Add eggs and vanilla; beat well. Add dry ingredients and milk alternately to beaten mixture and beat till well blended.

Spread batter in prepared pan. Bake in 350° oven about 20 minutes or till done. (Center will be slightly soft.) Cool on wire rack. Frost with Peanut Butter Frosting. Sprinkle with peanuts. Cut into bars. Makes 48.

Cereal Peanut Bars

½ cup light corn syrup
¼ cup packed brown sugar
1 cup peanut butter
1 teaspoon vanilla
2 cups crisp rice cereal
1 cup slightly crushed cornflakes
1 6-ounce package (1 cup)
    semisweet chocolate pieces

Butter a 9x9x2-inch baking pan. In saucepan combine corn syrup, brown sugar, and dash *salt*; bring to boiling. Stir in peanut butter; remove from heat. Stir in vanilla. Stir in rice cereal, corn flakes, and chocolate. Press into prepared pan. Cover and chill about 1 hour. Cut into bars; store in refrigerator. Makes 24.

Try making an assortment of inviting fresh-baked cookies for your family and friends. For variety, include bar cookies, drop cookies, and cutouts, such as (clockwise from top left) *Apricot Foldovers, Date Orange Bars, Lemon Squares, Chocolate Revel Bars, Double Chocolate Drops, Candy Window Sugar Cookies,* and *Peanut Butter Squares.* (See Index for recipe pages.)

Blonde Brownies

2 cups all-purpose flour
2 teaspoons baking powder
½ cup butter *or* margarine
2 cups packed brown sugar
2 eggs
1 teaspoon vanilla
1 cup chopped walnuts

Grease a 13x9x2-inch baking pan. Stir together flour, baking powder, and ¼ teaspoon *salt*. In saucepan melt butter or margarine; remove from heat. Stir in brown sugar. Add eggs and vanilla; beat till well blended. Stir dry ingredients and walnuts into brown sugar mixture. Spread batter in prepared pan. Bake in 350° oven for 20 to 25 minutes or till done. Cut into bars while warm. Makes 48.

Chocolate Chip Bars (pictured on page 56)

1¼ cups all-purpose flour
½ teaspoon baking powder
⅛ teaspoon baking soda
½ cup butter *or* margarine
¾ cup packed brown sugar
1 egg
2 tablespoons milk
1 teaspoon vanilla
1 6-ounce package (1 cup) semisweet chocolate pieces

Grease a 9x9x2-inch baking pan. Stir together flour, baking powder, baking soda, and ⅛ teaspoon *salt*. In mixer bowl beat butter or margarine on medium speed of electric mixer for 30 seconds. Add brown sugar and beat till fluffy. Add egg, milk, and vanilla; beat well.

Add dry ingredients to beaten mixture and beat till well blended. Stir in chocolate pieces. Spread batter in prepared pan. Bake in 350° oven about 30 minutes or till done. Cool on wire rack. Cut into bars. Makes 32.

Double Chocolate Crumble Bars

¾ cup all-purpose flour
2 tablespoons unsweetened cocoa powder
¼ teaspoon baking powder
½ cup butter *or* margarine
¾ cup sugar
2 eggs
1 teaspoon vanilla
½ cup chopped pecans
2 cups tiny marshmallows
1 6-ounce package (1 cup) semisweet chocolate pieces
1 cup peanut butter
1½ cups crisp rice cereal

Grease a 13x9x2-inch baking pan. Stir together flour, cocoa powder, baking powder, and ¼ teaspoon *salt*. In mixer bowl beat butter or margarine on medium speed of electric mixer for 30 seconds. Add sugar and beat till fluffy. Add eggs and vanilla; beat till well blended. Add dry ingredients to beaten mixture and beat till well blended. Stir in nuts. Spread batter in prepared pan. Bake in 350° oven for 15 to 20 minutes or till done. Sprinkle marshmallows evenly atop; bake 3 minutes more. Cool.

In small saucepan combine chocolate pieces and peanut butter; cook and stir over low heat till chocolate is melted. Stir in rice cereal. Spread chocolate mixture over marshmallow layer. Cover and chill. Cut into bars. Store in the refrigerator. Makes 48.

Almond Bars

This rich bar is like a pie with flaky pastry and a soft filling —

1 cup butter *or* margarine
2 cups all-purpose flour
½ cup water
1 8-ounce can almond paste
1 cup sugar
2 eggs
½ teaspoon vanilla

Cut butter into flour till mixture forms fine crumbs. Stir in water; mix well. Divide dough in half; wrap in waxed paper. Chill. Let dough stand at room temperature about 30 minutes till soft enough to handle before rolling out.

Meanwhile, in mixer bowl crumble almond paste. Add sugar, eggs, and vanilla; beat well. On lightly floured surface roll *each* half of dough into a 14x10-inch rectangle. Place half the dough in bottom and ½ inch up sides of an ungreased 13x9x2-inch baking pan. Spread with almond mixture. Cover with remaining dough; trim edges. Bake in 400° oven for 30 to 35 minutes. Cool. Cut into bars. Makes 48.

Lemon Squares (pictured on pages 72 and 73)

6 tablespoons butter
¼ cup sugar
¼ teaspoon salt
1 cup all-purpose flour
2 eggs
¾ cup sugar
¼ teaspoon finely shredded
    lemon peel
3 tablespoons lemon juice
2 tablespoons flour
¼ teaspoon baking powder

Grease an 8x8x2-inch baking pan. For cookie base, in mixer bowl beat butter on medium speed of electric mixer for 30 seconds. Add ¼ cup sugar and salt; beat till fluffy. Stir in 1 cup flour. Pat into bottom of pan. Bake in 350° oven about 15 minutes or till lightly browned.

Meanwhile, beat eggs. Add ¾ cup sugar, lemon peel, lemon juice, 2 tablespoons flour, and baking powder; beat about 3 minutes or till slightly thickened. Pour over baked layer. Bake in 350° oven for 25 to 30 minutes or till light brown around edges and set in center. Cool. Cut into squares. Sift with powdered sugar, if desired. Makes 36.

Old-Fashioned Raisin Bars

1¾ cups all-purpose flour
1 teaspoon baking soda
1 teaspoon ground cinnamon
½ teaspoon ground nutmeg
½ teaspoon ground allspice
¼ teaspoon ground cloves
1 cup raisins
½ cup shortening or cooking oil
1 cup sugar
1 beaten egg

Grease a 15x10x1-inch baking pan. Stir together flour, baking soda, cinnamon, nutmeg, allspice, cloves, and ¼ teaspoon *salt*. In saucepan combine raisins and 1 cup *water;* bring to boiling. Remove from heat; stir in shortening or cooking oil. Cool to lukewarm. Combine raisin mixture, sugar, and egg; beat well. Add dry ingredients to raisin mixture and beat till blended. If desired, stir in ½ cup chopped *nuts*. Turn into pan. Bake in 375° oven about 12 minutes or till done. Sift with powdered sugar or frost while warm, if desired. Cool. Cut into bars. Makes 48.

Raisin-Filled Granola Bars (pictured on pages 4 and 5)

½ cup sugar
1 tablespoon cornstarch
2 cups raisins
1 cup water
2 tablespoons lemon juice
2 cups all-purpose flour
½ teaspoon baking soda
¾ cup butter or margarine
1 cup packed brown sugar
1½ cups granola
2 tablespoons water

Grease and lightly flour a 13x9x2-inch baking pan. In saucepan combine sugar and cornstarch; stir in raisins and 1 cup water. Cook and stir over medium heat till thickened and bubbly. Remove from heat. Stir in lemon juice; cool. Stir together flour and baking soda. In mixer bowl beat butter with electric mixer for 30 seconds. Add brown sugar and beat till fluffy. Add dry ingredients to beaten mixture; beat well. Stir in granola and 2 tablespoons water.

Pat half the crumb mixture into pan; spread with raisin mixture. Sprinkle with remaining crumb mixture. Lightly press with hand. Bake in 350° oven for 30 to 35 minutes or till done. Cut into bars while warm. Cool. Makes 32.

Pecan Pie Bars (pictured on the cover)

1½ cups all-purpose flour
2 tablespoons brown sugar
6 tablespoons butter
2 eggs
½ cup packed brown sugar
½ cup chopped pecans
½ cup dark corn syrup
2 tablespoons butter, melted
1 teaspoon vanilla

Stir together flour and 2 tablespoons brown sugar; cut in the 6 tablespoons butter. Pat flour mixture into an ungreased 11x7x1½-inch baking pan. Bake in 350° oven for 15 minutes.

In mixing bowl beat eggs slightly; stir in ½ cup brown sugar, the pecans, corn syrup, 2 tablespoons melted butter, the vanilla, and ¼ teaspoon *salt*. Pour over baked layer. Bake in 350° oven about 25 minutes or till done. Cool slightly on wire rack; cut into bars. Makes 32.

Cheesecake Cookies (pictured on page 56)

1 cup all-purpose flour
⅓ cup packed brown sugar
6 tablespoons butter
1 8-ounce package cream cheese
¼ cup sugar
1 egg
2 tablespoons milk
¼ teaspoon grated lemon peel
2 tablespoons lemon juice
½ teaspoon vanilla
2 tablespoons chopped nuts

Stir together flour and brown sugar. Cut in butter till mixture resembles fine crumbs. Set aside 1 cup of the crumb mixture for topping. Press remaining mixture into bottom of an ungreased 8x8x2-inch baking pan. Bake in 350° oven for 15 minutes. In mixer bowl beat cream cheese on medium speed of electric mixer for 30 seconds. Add sugar; beat till fluffy. Add egg, milk, lemon peel, lemon juice, and vanilla; beat well. Spread over baked layer. Combine nuts and reserved 1 cup crumb mixture; sprinkle over cream cheese mixture. Bake in 350° oven for 20 to 25 minutes or till done. Cool on wire rack. Cut into bars. Makes 24.

Pumpkin Bars (pictured on pages 4 and 5)

2 cups all-purpose flour
2 teaspoons baking powder
2 teaspoons ground cinnamon
1 teaspoon baking soda
1 teaspoon salt
4 eggs
1 16-ounce can pumpkin
1½ cups sugar
1 cup cooking oil

Combine flour, baking powder, cinnamon, soda, and salt. Combine eggs, pumpkin, sugar, and oil; beat well. Add dry ingredients; beat well. Stir in ½ cup chopped *nuts*, if desired. Spread in ungreased 15x10x1-inch baking pan. Bake in 350° oven for 25 to 30 minutes or till done. Cool. If desired, frost with Cream Cheese Frosting (see recipe, page 5l); top with cinnamon-sugar. Cut into bars. Makes 36.

Zucchini Bars: Prepare Pumpkin Bars as above *except* substitute 2 cups shredded unpeeled *zucchini* for the canned pumpkin.

Date Orange Bars (pictured on pages 72 and 73)

1 cup all-purpose flour
½ teaspoon baking powder
¼ teaspoon baking soda
¼ cup butter *or* margarine
½ cup packed brown sugar
1 egg
1 teaspoon grated orange peel
¼ cup milk
¼ cup orange juice
½ cup pitted whole dates, snipped
½ cup chopped walnuts

Grease an 11x7x1½-inch baking pan. Stir together flour, baking powder, and baking soda. In mixer bowl beat butter or margarine on medium speed of electric mixer for 30 seconds. Add brown sugar and beat till fluffy. Add egg and orange peel; beat well. Combine milk and orange juice.

Add dry ingredients and milk mixture alternately to beaten mixture and beat till well blended. Stir in dates and walnuts. Spread batter in prepared pan. Bake in 350° oven about 25 minutes or till done. Cool on wire rack. Spread with Powdered Sugar Icing, if desired (see recipe, page 52). Cut into bars. Makes 24.

Seven-Layer Bars

½ cup butter *or* margarine
1½ cups crushed graham crackers
1 6-ounce package (1 cup) semisweet chocolate pieces
1 6-ounce package (1 cup) butterscotch pieces
1 3½-ounce can flaked coconut
½ cup chopped walnuts
1 14-ounce can (1¼ cups) *sweetened condensed* milk

In saucepan melt butter; stir in graham crackers. Pat mixture evenly into bottom of an ungreased 13x9x2-inch baking pan. Layer in order chocolate pieces, butterscotch pieces, coconut, and walnuts. Pour sweetened condensed milk evenly over all. Bake in 350° oven about 30 minutes or till done. Cool on wire rack. Cut into bars. Makes 36.

Festive & Fancy Cookies

Springerle (see recipe, page 82), *Lemon Rounds* (see recipe, page 87), and *Viennese Butter Rounds* (see recipe, page 80)

Cutout Cookies

Cutout cookies seem to brighten holiday celebrations and add a festive touch to everyday occasions. Their dough—rolled thin or thick—can be cut into circles, squares, or other cookie cutter shapes, then filled, frosted, or decorated.

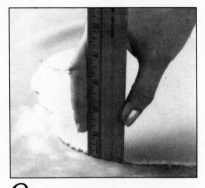

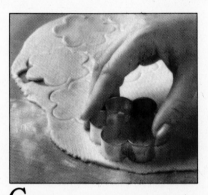

*W*rap prepared cookie dough in clear plastic wrap or foil. Chill dough in the refrigerator to make it firm and easy to roll. Dough can be chilled overnight. If too stiff, let dough stand at room temperature a few minutes before handling. If dough becomes too soft during rolling, chill again or sprinkle more flour on rolling surface.

*O*n a lightly floured surface, roll out dough from the center to the edges, measuring the thickness. If you do much rerolling of dough for cutout cookies, try rolling it on a surface dusted with a mixture of equal parts flour and powdered sugar. The cookies won't be as tough as when rerolled in flour alone.

*C*ut dough into shapes using floured cookie cutters, a sharp knife, or fluted pastry wheel. Or, use cardboard pattern, tracing around edges with a sharp knife. Cut cookies as close together as possible. Use a pancake turner or wide metal spatula to remove them from floured surface. Reroll any extra dough to cut as above.

Rolled Sugar Cookies (candy window variation pictured on pages 72 and 73)

Frost and decorate basic cutout cookies, if desired. See Frostings and Fillings *chapter for ideas* —

- **2 cups all-purpose flour**
- **1½ teaspoons baking powder**
- **¼ teaspoon salt**
- **6 tablespoons butter *or* margarine**
- **⅓ cup shortening**
- **¾ cup sugar**
- **1 egg**
- **1 tablespoon milk**
- **1 teaspoon vanilla**

Stir together flour, baking powder, and salt. Beat butter and shortening with electric mixer for 30 seconds. Add sugar and beat till fluffy. Add egg, milk, and vanilla; beat well. Add dry ingredients; beat well. Divide dough in half; cover and chill about 3 hours. Working with half of the dough at a time, on lightly floured surface roll to ⅛-inch thickness. Cut into desired shapes. Place on ungreased cookie sheet. Bake in 375° oven for 7 to 8 minutes or till done. Remove to wire rack; cool. Makes 36 to 48.

Sour Cream Sugar Cookies: Prepare Rolled Sugar Cookies dough as above *except* use ¼ cup *dairy sour cream* instead of milk.

Candy Window Sugar Cookies: Prepare Rolled Sugar Cookies dough as above. Roll out and cut into desired shapes; place on foil-lined cookie sheet. Cut out small shape (1 to 1¼ inches) in center of each. Crush 3 ounces *hard sour candy;* place about ½ teaspoon in each center. Bake as directed till candy melts. Peel off foil; cool.

Gingerbread Cutouts

5 cups all-purpose flour
2 teaspoons ground ginger
1½ teaspoons baking soda
1 teaspoon ground cinnamon
1 teaspoon ground cloves
1 cup shortening
1 cup sugar
1 egg
1 cup molasses
2 tablespoons vinegar

Combine flour, ginger, soda, cinnamon, cloves, and ½ teaspoon *salt*. In mixer bowl beat shortening on medium speed of electric mixer for 30 seconds. Add sugar; beat till fluffy. Add egg, molasses, and vinegar; beat well. Add dry ingredients to beaten mixture and beat till well blended. Divide dough into thirds. Cover; chill about 3 hours.

Working with ⅓ of the dough at a time, on lightly floured surface roll to ⅛-inch thickness. Cut into desired shapes. Place on a greased cookie sheet. Bake in 375° oven for 5 to 6 minutes or till done. Cool about 1 minute; remove to wire rack. Cool. Decorate, if desired. Makes about 60.

Rolled Spice Cookies

4 cups all-purpose flour
2 teaspoons ground cinnamon
1 teaspoon ground nutmeg
½ teaspoon ground cloves
¼ teaspoon baking soda
1½ cups butter *or* margarine
2 cups packed brown sugar
1 egg

Stir together flour, cinnamon, nutmeg, cloves, and baking soda. In mixer bowl beat butter or margarine on medium speed of electric mixer for 30 seconds. Add brown sugar and beat till fluffy. Add egg; beat well. Add dry ingredients to beaten mixture and beat till well blended.

Cover and chill about 2 hours. On lightly floured surface, roll dough to ⅛-inch thickness. Cut into desired shapes. Place on ungreased cookie sheet. Bake in 350° oven for 8 to 10 minutes or till done. Cool about 1 minute before removing to wire rack; cool. Decorate, if desired. Makes about 72.

Peanut Butter Cutouts

1¾ cups all-purpose flour
¾ teaspoon baking soda
¼ teaspoon salt
½ cup shortening
½ cup peanut butter
½ cup sugar
½ cup packed brown sugar
1 egg
2 tablespoons milk
1 teaspoon finely shredded
orange peel (optional)

Stir together flour, baking soda, and salt. In mixer bowl beat shortening and peanut butter on medium speed of electric mixer for 30 seconds. Add sugar and brown sugar; beat till fluffy. Add egg, milk, and orange peel; beat well. Add dry ingredients to beaten mixture and beat till well blended. Cover and chill about 3 hours.

On lightly floured surface, roll dough to ⅛-inch thickness; cut into desired shapes. Place on an ungreased cookie sheet. Bake in 350° oven about 8 minutes or till done. Remove to wire rack; cool. Makes about 48.

Scotch Shortbread

1 cup butter *or* margarine
¼ cup sugar
½ teaspoon vanilla
2½ cups all-purpose flour

Beat together butter, sugar, and vanilla with electric mixer till light and fluffy. Stir in flour. Divide dough in half. On lightly floured surface, roll to ½-inch thickness. Cut into 2x½-inch strips or cut into 1¾-inch rounds with floured cutter. Place on ungreased cookie sheet. (Or, on ungreased cookie sheet pat each half into a 7-inch circle. With fork, prick dough deeply to make 16 pie-shaped wedges.) Bake in 325° oven for 20 to 25 minutes or till done. Cool 1 minute; remove and cool. Makes about 32.

Viennese Butter Rounds (pictured on page 77)

1 cup all-purpose flour
½ cup ground pecans
⅓ cup sugar
½ cup butter *or* margarine
⅔ cup sifted powdered sugar
¼ cup butter *or* margarine, softened
1 square (1 ounce) unsweetened chocolate, melted and cooled
⅓ cup apricot preserves

Combine flour, pecans, and sugar. Beat ½ cup butter for 30 seconds. Add flour mixture; beat till blended. On floured surface, roll dough to ¹/₁₆-inch thickness. Cut with floured scalloped cutter. (If desired, cut out center of *half* the cookies using a small cutter.) Place on ungreased cookie sheet. Bake in 375° oven for 5 to 6 minutes or till done. Cool 1 minute; remove. Cool. Combine powdered sugar, ¼ cup softened butter, and chocolate; beat well.

Spread chocolate mixture on bottoms of half the cookies (use cookies without cutout centers). Spread apricot preserves over chocolate mixture. Place remaining cookies atop preserves; press lightly. Makes about 30.

Coconut Sugar Cookies

1¾ cups all-purpose flour
1½ teaspoons baking powder
¼ teaspoon salt
¾ cup butter *or* margarine
⅔ cup sugar
2 eggs
¼ teaspoon almond extract
1 cup grated coconut

Combine flour, baking powder, and salt. Beat butter for 30 seconds. Add sugar and beat till fluffy. Add eggs and almond extract; beat well. Add dry ingredients; beat till blended. Stir in coconut. Cover; chill about 4 hours.

On lightly floured surface, roll dough to ¼-inch thickness. Cut into desired shapes. Place on ungreased cookie sheet. Bake in 375° oven about 8 minutes or till done. Remove to wire rack; cool. Decorate, if desired. Makes about 36.

Jam-Filled Cookies

2¾ cups all-purpose flour
½ teaspoon baking soda
½ teaspoon cream of tartar
1 cup butter *or* margarine
½ cup sugar
½ cup sifted powdered sugar
1 egg
1½ teaspoons vanilla
½ cup jam
1 tablespoon cornstarch
1 tablespoon water

Stir together flour, soda, and cream of tartar. Beat butter for 30 seconds. Add sugar and powdered sugar; beat till fluffy. Add egg and vanilla; beat well. Add dry ingredients and beat till blended. Cover; chill about 1 hour. Meanwhile, for filling, combine jam and cornstarch; stir in water. Cook and stir till thick; cool. On lightly floured surface, roll dough to ⅛-inch thickness.

Cut with floured scalloped cookie cutter. Place a scant ½ *teaspoon* filling in center of *half* the cookies. Cut out small shape in center of remaining cookies. Place cookies over filling; press lightly to seal. Bake in 350° oven for 10 to 12 minutes or till done. Remove; cool. Makes about 40.

Sherry Almond Rounds

1½ cups all-purpose flour
¼ teaspoon salt
½ cup butter *or* margarine
1 cup sifted powdered sugar
3 tablespoons dry sherry
½ teaspoon vanilla
½ cup finely chopped almonds, toasted
1 slightly beaten egg
2 tablespoons water

Combine flour and salt. Beat butter for 30 seconds. Add powdered sugar and beat till fluffy. Add sherry and vanilla; beat well. Add dry ingredients and beat till blended. Stir in nuts. Flatten dough between 2 sheets of lightly floured waxed paper; roll to ¼-inch thickness.

Remove top sheet; cut with floured scalloped cutter. Remove from paper; place on ungreased cookie sheet. Combine egg and water; brush over cookies. Sprinkle with sugar or colored sugar, if desired. Bake in 375° oven about 10 minutes or till done. Remove; cool. Makes about 36.

At your next party serve an assortment of delicious cookies including *Jam-Filled Cookies, Orange Drop Cookies* (see recipe, page 62), and *Peanut Blossoms* (see recipe, page 84).

Apricot Foldovers (pictured on pages 72 and 73)

1 **cup shredded American cheese
   (4 ounces)**
½ **cup butter** *or* **margarine**
1⅓ **cups all-purpose flour**
2 **tablespoons water**
1 **cup dried apricots, cut up**
1 **cup sugar**
   Milk

In mixer bowl beat cheese and butter or margarine till light. Add flour and beat till well blended. Add water; beat well. Divide dough in half. Cover and chill for 4 to 5 hours. For filling, in saucepan cook apricots according to package directions; drain well. Stir sugar into hot fruit.

Cook and stir till mixture boils; cool. Working with half the dough at a time, on lightly floured surface roll into a 10-inch square. Cut into sixteen 2½-inch squares. Place about *1 teaspoon* apricot filling on each square. Fold over diagonally; seal with tines of a fork. Place on ungreased cookie sheet. Brush with a little milk; sprinkle with additional sugar, if desired. Bake in 375° oven for 8 to 10 minutes or till done. Remove to wire rack; cool. Makes 32.

Lebkuchen (pictured on pages 4 and 5)

3 **cups all-purpose flour**
1¼ **teaspoons ground nutmeg**
1¼ **teaspoons ground cinnamon**
½ **teaspoon baking soda**
½ **teaspoon ground cloves**
½ **teaspoon ground allspice**
1 **egg**
¾ **cup packed brown sugar**
½ **cup honey**
½ **cup dark molasses**
½ **cup slivered almonds**
½ **cup diced mixed candied fruits
   and peels, finely chopped**
   Lemon Glaze (optional)

Stir together flour, nutmeg, cinnamon, soda, cloves, and allspice. In mixer bowl beat egg; add brown sugar and beat on medium speed of electric mixer till fluffy. Stir in honey and molasses. Add dry ingredients to molasses mixture; beat till well blended. Stir in nuts and fruits and peels.

Cover; chill for several hours. On floured surface roll dough into a 14-inch square. Cut into 3½x2-inch rectangles. Place 2 inches apart on a greased cookie sheet. Bake in 375° oven for 12 to 14 minutes or till done. Cool about 1 minute; remove to wire rack. While cookies are warm, brush with Lemon Glaze, if desired. Makes 28.

Lemon Glaze: Combine 1 slightly beaten *egg white,* 1½ cups sifted *powdered sugar,* ½ teaspoon grated *lemon peel,* 1 tablespoon *lemon juice,* and dash *salt;* beat well.

Springerle (pictured on page 77)

*This Scandinavian cutout cookie puffs up
when baked and becomes very firm —*

4 **cups all-purpose flour**
1 **teaspoon baking soda**
4 **eggs**
4¾ **cups sifted powdered sugar
   (1 pound)**
20 **drops oil of anise**
1½ **to 2 teaspoons aniseed,
   crushed**

Combine flour and baking soda. In large mixer bowl beat eggs with electric mixer till light. Gradually beat in powdered sugar; continue beating on high speed about 15 minutes or till like soft meringue. Stir in oil of anise. Add about ¾ of the flour mixture and beat on low speed till blended. By hand, stir in remaining flour mixture. Cover with foil; let stand about 15 minutes. Divide dough into thirds.

On lightly floured surface, roll each portion into an 8-inch square. Let stand for 1 minute. Dust springerle mold or rolling pin with additional flour; roll or press hard enough on dough to make a clear design. With sharp knife cut cookies apart. Place on lightly floured surface; cover with a towel and let stand 6 hours or overnight. Sprinkle greased cookie sheet with crushed aniseed. Brush excess flour from cookies. With finger, rub bottom of each cookie lightly with cold water. Place on prepared cookie sheet. Bake in 300° oven about 18 minutes or till a light straw color. Remove to wire rack; cool. Makes about 72.

Note: To soften slightly, store cookies with a quartered apple in an airtight container at room temperature for a few days.

Shaped Cookies

The final form of shaped cookies depends on whether the dough was shaped by hand or forced through a cookie press. Dough rolled into balls can be shaped further by flattening the ball, making crisscross marks with a fork, or making a thumbprint.

*F*latten dough shaped into balls by dipping the bottom of a glass in sugar and pressing the dough with the glass bottom, as shown. (To get sugar to stick, first press the bottom of glass in cookie dough.) For light-colored cookies use colored sugar or cinnamon-sugar.

*A*nother way to flatten the ball of dough is to use the tines of a fork. If desired, dip the fork in sugar. Make fork marks in one direction, as shown, or crisscross the markings for a different pattern.

*T*o form pressed cookies, choose desired plate and insert into cookie press, according to manufacturer's directions. Pack dough into press; hold upright over cookie sheet, as shown. Press out dough, then give handle a slight turn in reverse to stop dough; lift off press. To make long strips, hold press at an angle.

Ginger Crinkles

2¼ **cups all-purpose flour**
2 **teaspoons baking soda**
1 **teaspoon ground ginger**
1 **teaspoon ground cinnamon**
½ **teaspoon ground cloves**
1 **cup packed brown sugar**
¾ **cup shortening *or* cooking oil**
¼ **cup molasses**
1 **egg**

Stir together flour, baking soda, ginger, cinnamon, cloves, and ¼ teaspoon *salt*. In mixer bowl combine brown sugar, shortening or cooking oil, molasses, and egg; beat well. Add dry ingredients to beaten mixture and beat till well blended.

Shape into 1-inch balls. Roll in sugar, if desired. Place 2 inches apart on an ungreased cookie sheet. Bake in 375° oven about 10 minutes or till done. Remove from cookie sheet; cool on wire rack. Makes about 48.

Sandies (pictured on the cover)

1 **cup butter *or* margarine**
⅓ **cup sugar**
2 **teaspoons vanilla**
2 **cups all-purpose flour**
1 **cup chopped pecans**
¼ **cup powdered sugar**

Beat butter for 30 seconds. Add sugar; beat till fluffy. Add 2 teaspoons *water* and vanilla; beat well. Stir in flour and nuts. Shape into 1-inch balls or 1½x½-inch fingers.

Place on ungreased cookie sheet. Bake in 325° oven about 20 minutes. Cool thoroughly. In plastic bag gently shake a few at a time in powdered sugar. Makes about 36.

Peanut Butter Cookies (also pictured on pages 4 and 5)

1¼ **cups all-purpose flour**
¾ **teaspoon baking soda**
¼ **teaspoon salt**
½ **cup butter** *or* **margarine**
½ **cup peanut butter**
½ **cup sugar**
½ **cup packed brown sugar**
1 **egg**
½ **teaspoon vanilla**

Stir together flour, soda, and salt. Beat butter and peanut butter for 30 seconds. Add sugar and brown sugar; beat till fluffy. Add egg and vanilla; beat well. Add dry ingredients to beaten mixture and beat till well blended.

Shape dough into 1-inch balls; roll in additional sugar, if desired. Place on ungreased cookie sheet. Press crisscross markings with a fork. Bake in 375° oven about 10 minutes or till done. Cool 1 minute; remove to rack. Cool. Makes about 48.

Double Peanut Cookies: Prepare Peanut Butter Cookies as above *except* stir in 1 cup chopped *salted peanuts.*

Peanut Blossoms (pictured on page 8l)

1¾ **cups all-purpose flour**
1 **teaspoon baking powder**
¼ **teaspoon salt**
⅛ **teaspoon baking soda**
½ **cup butter** *or* **margarine**
½ **cup peanut butter**
½ **cup sugar**
½ **cup packed brown sugar**
1 **egg**
2 **tablespoons milk**
1 **teaspoon vanilla**
Milk chocolate stars

Stir together flour, baking powder, salt, and baking soda. In mixer bowl beat butter or margarine and peanut butter on medium speed of electric mixer for 30 seconds. Add sugar and brown sugar; beat till fluffy. Add egg, milk, and vanilla; beat well. Add dry ingredients and beat till well blended.

If necessary, cover and chill about 1 hour for easier handling. Shape dough into 1-inch balls; roll in additional sugar. Place on ungreased cookie sheet. Bake in 375° oven for 10 to 12 minutes or till done. Immediately press a chocolate candy atop each cookie. Remove to wire rack; cool. Makes about 64.

Chocolate Crinkles

2 **cups all-purpose flour**
2 **teaspoons baking powder**
1½ **cups sugar**
½ **cup cooking oil**
4 **squares (4 ounces) unsweetened chocolate, melted and cooled**
2 **teaspoons vanilla**
3 **eggs**
Sifted powdered sugar

Stir together flour and baking powder. In mixer bowl stir together sugar, oil, melted chocolate, and vanilla. Beat in eggs. Add dry ingredients to chocolate mixture and beat till blended. Cover and chill. Using 1 tablespoon dough for each, shape into balls; roll in powdered sugar.

Place on a greased cookie sheet. Bake in 375° oven for 10 to 12 minutes or till done. While cookies are warm, roll again in powdered sugar, if desired. Cool. Makes about 48.

Oatmeal Cookies

1 **cup all-purpose flour**
½ **teaspoon baking powder**
½ **teaspoon baking soda**
¼ **cup shortening**
¼ **cup butter** *or* **margarine**
½ **cup sugar**
⅓ **cup packed brown sugar**
1 **egg**
2 **tablespoons milk**
½ **teaspoon vanilla**
1 **cup quick-cooking rolled oats**

Stir together flour, baking powder, baking soda, and ¼ teaspoon *salt*. In mixer bowl beat shortening and butter on medium speed of electric mixer for 30 seconds. Add sugar and brown sugar and beat till fluffy. Add egg, milk, and vanilla; beat well. Add dry ingredients to beaten mixture and beat till well blended. Stir in oats.

Stir in ¼ cup chopped *walnuts,* if desired. Cover; chill about 2 hours. Shape into 1-inch balls. Dip tops of balls in additional sugar, if desired. Place on an ungreased cookie sheet. Bake in 375° oven for 10 to 12 minutes or till done. Remove from cookie sheet; cool on wire rack. Makes about 36.

These shaped cookies are *Chocolate Crinkles, Kringla* (see recipe, page 86),
Almond Cookies (see recipe, page 87), *Peanut Butter Cookies,* and *Spritz* (see recipe, page 89).

Oatmeal Molasses Cookies

1½　**cups all-purpose flour**
1　**teaspoon baking soda**
1　**teaspoon ground ginger**
½　**teaspoon salt**
¼　**teaspoon ground cloves**
½　**cup shortening**
1　**cup sugar**
1　**egg**
¼　**cup molasses**
¾　**cup quick-cooking rolled oats**

Stir together flour, baking soda, ginger, salt, and cloves. In mixer bowl beat shortening on medium speed of electric mixer for 30 seconds. Add sugar and beat till fluffy. Add egg and molasses; beat well. Add dry ingredients to beaten mixture and beat till well blended.

Stir in oats. Using a rounded teaspoon for each, shape into balls. Place on an ungreased cookie sheet. Bake in 375° oven about 10 minutes or till done. Cool about 1 minute before removing to wire rack. Cool. Makes about 36.

Shaped Sugar Cookies

2　**cups all-purpose flour**
½　**teaspoon cream of tartar**
¼　**teaspoon baking soda**
¼　**teaspoon salt**
1　**cup butter** *or* **margarine**
1　**cup sugar**
1　**egg**
1　**teaspoon vanilla**
　Sugar *or* **colored sugar**

Stir together flour, cream of tartar, baking soda, and salt. Beat butter for 30 seconds. Add 1 cup sugar and beat till fluffy. Add egg and vanilla; beat well. Add dry ingredients to beaten mixture and beat till blended.

Shape into 1-inch balls. Place on ungreased cookie sheet. Dip bottom of a glass in additional sugar or colored sugar; use glass to flatten cookies. Bake in 375° oven for 8 to 10 minutes or till done. Remove from cookie sheet; cool on wire rack. Makes about 54.

Snickerdoodles　(pictured on page 88)

3¾　**cups all-purpose flour**
½　**teaspoon baking soda**
½　**teaspoon cream of tartar**
1　**cup butter** *or* **margarine**
2　**cups sugar**
2　**eggs**
¼　**cup milk**
1　**teaspoon vanilla**
3　**tablespoons sugar**
1　**teaspoon ground cinnamon**

Stir together flour, baking soda, cream of tartar, and ½ teaspoon *salt*. In mixer bowl beat butter with electric mixer for 30 seconds. Add the 2 cups sugar and beat till fluffy. Add eggs, milk, and vanilla; beat well. Add dry ingredients to beaten mixture and beat till well blended.

Shape into 1-inch balls; roll in a mixture of 3 tablespoons sugar and cinnamon. Place on a greased cookie sheet. Flatten slightly with bottom of a glass. Bake in 375° oven about 8 minutes or till done. Remove from cookie sheet; cool on wire rack. Makes about 66.

Kringla　(pictured on page 85)

3　**cups all-purpose flour**
2½　**teaspoons baking powder**
1　**teaspoon baking soda**
½　**teaspoon salt**
¼　**teaspoon ground nutmeg** *or*
　　cardamom (optional)
½　**cup butter** *or* **margarine**
1　**cup sugar**
1　**egg**
1　**teaspoon vanilla**
¾　**cup buttermilk**

Combine flour, baking powder, soda, salt, and nutmeg or cardamom. Beat butter for 30 seconds. Add sugar; beat till fluffy. Add egg and vanilla; beat well. Alternately add dry ingredients and buttermilk, beating till well blended. Cover; chill about 2 hours. Divide in half. Working with half at a time, on floured surface roll into a 10x5-inch rectangle.

With sharp knife, cut into twenty 5x½-inch strips. Roll each strip with hands to form a 10-inch-long rope. Shape into a loop, crossing 1½ inches from ends of rope. Twist rope at crossing point. Fold loop over to ends and seal, forming a pretzel shape. Place on ungreased cookie sheet. Bake in 425° oven about 5 minutes or till lightly browned on bottom (tops will be pale). Remove; cool. Makes 40.

Jam Thumbprints (pictured on page 88 and the cover)

1½ cups all-purpose flour
⅔ cup butter *or* margarine
⅓ cup sugar
2 egg yolks
1 teaspoon vanilla
1 slightly beaten egg white
¾ cup finely chopped walnuts
⅓ cup red raspberry *or* apricot
  preserves

Stir together flour and ¼ teaspoon *salt*. In mixer bowl beat butter for 30 seconds. Add sugar and beat till fluffy. Add egg yolks and vanilla; beat well. Add dry ingredients to beaten mixture and beat till well blended. Cover; chill about 1 hour. Shape into 1-inch balls; roll in egg white, then in nuts. Place on an ungreased cookie sheet. Press down centers with thumb. Bake in 350° oven for 15 to 17 minutes or till done. Remove to wire rack; cool. Just before serving, fill the centers with preserves. Makes about 36.

Almond Cookies (pictured on page 85)

2¾ cups all-purpose flour
1 cup sugar
½ teaspoon baking soda
1 cup butter *or* margarine
1 slightly beaten egg
2 tablespoons milk
1 teaspoon almond extract
24 blanched almonds, halved

In mixing bowl stir together flour, sugar, soda, and ½ teaspoon *salt*. Cut in butter or margarine till mixture resembles fine crumbs. Combine egg, milk, and almond extract. Add to flour mixture; mix well. Shape dough into 1-inch balls. Place 2 inches apart on an ungreased cookie sheet.
  Place an almond half atop each ball of dough and press to flatten slightly. Bake in 325° oven for 16 to 18 minutes or till done. Remove to wire rack; cool. Makes about 48.

Lemon Rounds (pictured on page 77)

1 cup butter *or* margarine
½ cup sifted powdered sugar
½ teaspoon finely shredded
  lemon peel
1 tablespoon lemon juice
1 teaspoon vanilla
2½ cups all-purpose flour
½ cup finely chopped pecans
  Lemon Icing (optional)

Beat butter for 30 seconds. Add powdered sugar; beat till fluffy. Stir in lemon peel, lemon juice, and vanilla. Stir in flour, mixing well. Shape dough into 1-inch balls. Dip one side in chopped nuts. Place nut side up on ungreased cookie sheet. Flatten to ¼-inch thickness with bottom of a glass. Bake in 350° oven for 12 to 15 minutes. Remove; cool. Drizzle with Lemon Icing, if desired. Makes about 60.
  Lemon Icing: Combine 1 cup sifted *powdered sugar* and enough *lemon juice* (3 to 4 teaspoons) to make of drizzling consistency.

Candy Cane Cookies

2 cups all-purpose flour
½ teaspoon salt
¼ teaspoon baking powder
¾ cup butter *or* margarine
¾ cup sugar
1 egg
½ teaspoon vanilla
½ teaspoon peppermint extract
⅓ cup flaked coconut
1 teaspoon red food coloring

Stir together flour, salt, and baking powder. In mixer bowl beat butter for 30 seconds. Add sugar and beat till fluffy. Add egg, vanilla, and peppermint extract; beat well. Add dry ingredients to beaten mixture and beat till well blended. Divide dough in half. Stir coconut into one half; stir food coloring into remaining dough. Cover; chill about 30 minutes. Divide each portion of dough into 30 balls; keep half the balls of each portion chilled till ready to use.
  With hands, roll each ball into a 5-inch-long rope. For each cane, pinch together one end of a white rope and one end of a red rope; twist together. Pinch ropes together at remaining end. Place on ungreased cookie sheet; curve one end to form a cane. Bake in 375° oven about 10 minutes or till done. Cool about 2 minutes before removing to wire rack. Cool thoroughly. Makes 30.

For a variety of shaped cookie forms, include *Pecan Tassies, Pineapple-Filled Spritz, Snickerdoodles* (see recipe, page 86), and *Jam Thumbprints* (see recipe, page 87).

Spritz (pictured on page 85; variation pictured opposite)

Sprinkle unbaked Spritz cookies with colored sugar, ground nuts, or decorative candies —

3½ **cups all-purpose flour**
1 **teaspoon baking powder**
1½ **cups butter *or* margarine**
1 **cup sugar**
1 **egg**
1 **teaspoon vanilla**
½ **teaspoon almond extract (optional)**

Stir together flour and baking powder. Beat butter for 30 seconds. Add sugar and beat till fluffy. Add egg, vanilla, and almond extract, if desired; beat well. Gradually add dry ingredients to beaten mixture and beat till well blended. Do not chill. Force dough through cookie press onto an ungreased cookie sheet. Decorate, if desired. Bake in 400° oven for 7 to 8 minutes or till done. Remove; cool. Makes about 60.

Pineapple-Filled Spritz: Prepare Spritz dough as above. Using a ribbon plate and ⅓ of the dough, press onto an ungreased cookie sheet into eight 10-inch strips. Using a star plate and another ⅓ of the dough, press lengthwise rows of dough on top of each strip, making a rim along both edges. Spoon *Pineapple Filling* between rims atop strips. Bake in 400° oven for 8 to 10 minutes or till done. While strips are hot, cut into 1¼-inch diagonals. Press the remaining dough into desired shapes and bake as directed above for Spritz.

Pineapple Filling: In saucepan stir together one 20-ounce can *crushed pineapple,* drained, and ⅔ cup *sugar.* Bring to boiling; reduce heat and simmer for 30 to 35 minutes or till mixture is very thick, stirring often. Using a few drops of food coloring, tint portions of the filling green or red, if desired. Cool thoroughly.

Mocha Logs

2¼ **cups all-purpose flour**
½ **teaspoon salt**
¼ **teaspoon baking powder**
2 **tablespoons instant coffee crystals**
1 **teaspoon water**
1 **cup butter *or* margarine**
¾ **cup sugar**
1 **egg**
1 **teaspoon vanilla**
4 **squares (4 ounces) semisweet chocolate, melted**
⅔ **cup finely chopped pecans**

Stir together flour, salt, and baking powder. In mixer bowl combine coffee crystals and water, stirring till dissolved. Add butter or margarine; beat on medium speed of electric mixer for 30 seconds. Add sugar and beat till fluffy. Add egg and vanilla; beat well. Add dry ingredients to beaten mixture and beat till well blended.

Pack dough, half at a time, into cookie press with star plate inserted. Force through press onto ungreased cookie sheet into 3-inch-long strips. Bake in 375° oven for 8 to 10 minutes or till done. Remove; cool on wire rack. Dip top of one end of each cookie in chocolate; coat with nuts. Place cookies in refrigerator for a few minutes till chocolate becomes firm. Makes about 80.

Pecan Tassies

½ **cup butter *or* margarine**
1 **3-ounce package cream cheese**
1 **cup all-purpose flour**
1 **egg**
¾ **cup packed brown sugar**
1 **tablespoon butter *or* margarine, softened**
1 **teaspoon vanilla**
 Dash salt
½ **cup coarsely chopped pecans**

For pastry, in mixer bowl beat the ½ cup butter or margarine and the cream cheese. Add flour; beat well. If dough is too soft, cover and chill 1 hour. In mixer bowl stir together egg, brown sugar, the 1 tablespoon butter, the vanilla, and salt just till smooth; set aside.

Shape chilled pastry into 2 dozen 1-inch balls; place each ball in an ungreased 1¾-inch muffin cup. Press dough into bottom and sides of cups. Spoon about 1 teaspoon of the chopped pecans into each pastry-lined muffin cup; fill each with egg mixture. Bake in 325° oven about 25 minutes or till filling is set. Cool; remove from pans. Store, covered, in refrigerator. Makes 24.

Start with Cookie Mix

Homemade Cookie Mix

4 cups all-purpose flour
1 cup sugar
1 cup packed brown sugar
2 teaspoons baking powder
1½ teaspoons salt
1⅓ cups shortening that does not
    require refrigeration

In large mixing bowl stir together flour, sugar, brown sugar, baking powder, and salt. Cut in shortening till mixture resembles fine crumbs. Store in covered container up to 6 weeks at room temperature. For longer storage, place in freezer. To measure, lightly spoon mix into measuring cup; level with spatula. Makes about 8½ cups.

Chocolate Drops

2¼ cups Homemade Cookie Mix
1 egg
¼ cup milk
2 squares (2 ounces)
    unsweetened chocolate,
    melted and cooled
½ cup semisweet chocolate
    pieces

In mixing bowl combine Homemade Cookie Mix, egg, and milk; beat well. Stir in unsweetened chocolate, then chocolate pieces. Stir in ½ cup chopped *nuts,* if desired.
Drop from a teaspoon 2 inches apart onto a greased cookie sheet. Bake in 375° oven for 8 to 10 minutes or till done. Remove to wire rack; cool. Makes about 30.

Oatmeal Raisin Cookies

2½ cups Homemade Cookie Mix
¼ cup packed brown sugar
½ teaspoon ground cinnamon
½ teaspoon ground nutmeg
2 eggs
½ cup milk
1 cup quick-cooking rolled oats
1 cup raisins

In mixing bowl stir together Homemade Cookie Mix, brown sugar, cinnamon, and nutmeg. Add eggs and milk; beat well. Stir in oats and raisins. Cover and let stand 30 minutes, or refrigerate till ready to use.
Drop from a teaspoon 2 inches apart onto a greased cookie sheet. Bake in 375° oven for 8 to 10 minutes or till done. Remove to wire rack; cool. Makes about 36.

Orange Coconut Drops

2½ cups Homemade Cookie Mix
¼ cup orange marmalade
1 egg
3 tablespoons orange juice
1 cup coconut
    Orange Butter Frosting (see
    recipe, page 50) (optional)

In mixing bowl stir together Homemade Cookie Mix, orange marmalade, egg, and orange juice; beat well. Stir in coconut. Drop from a teaspoon 2 inches apart onto a greased cookie sheet. Bake in 350° oven for 8 to 10 minutes or till done. Remove to wire rack; cool. If desired, frost with Orange Butter Frosting. Makes about 30.

Peanut Molasses Cookies

2 cups Homemade Cookie Mix
1 egg
½ cup chopped peanuts
¼ cup molasses

Beat together Homemade Cookie Mix, egg, peanuts, molasses, and 2 tablespoons *water.* Drop from teaspoon onto ungreased cookie sheet. Bake in 375° oven for 8 to 10 minutes. Cool 1 minute; remove to rack. Cool. Makes about 30.

Granola Raisin Bars

2 cups Homemade Cookie Mix
1 egg
½ cup milk
½ teaspoon vanilla
1 cup granola
½ cup raisins
2 tablespoons butter *or* margarine, melted

Grease a 9x9x2-inch or an 8x8x2-inch baking pan. In mixing bowl stir together Homemade Cookie Mix, egg, milk, and vanilla; beat well. Stir in *half* of the granola and the raisins.

Spread batter in prepared pan. Stir together remaining granola and melted butter or margarine; sprinkle over top. Bake in 350° oven for 20 to 25 minutes or till done. Cool on wire rack. Cut into bars. Makes 24.

Mince Oatmeal Bars

2 cups Homemade Cookie Mix
¾ cup quick-cooking rolled oats
1 beaten egg
1 tablespoon water
1 cup prepared mincemeat

Grease a 9x9x2-inch baking pan. In mixing bowl stir together Homemade Cookie Mix, oats, egg, and water; pat *about 2 cups* of the oat mixture into prepared pan. Spoon mincemeat over base; crumble remaining oat mixture on top. Bake in 350° oven for 30 to 35 minutes or till done. Cool on wire rack. Cut into bars. Makes 24.

Homemade Brownie Mix

Also use this mix to make the layered bar cookies in next recipe —

5 cups sugar
3 cups all-purpose flour
2 cups unsweetened cocoa powder
1 tablespoon baking powder
1 tablespoon salt
3½ cups shortening that does not require refrigeration

In large mixing bowl stir together sugar, flour, cocoa powder, baking powder, and salt. Cut in shortening till mixture resembles evenly distributed, coarse crumbs. Store in covered container up to 6 weeks at room temperature. For longer storage, place in freezer. To measure, pack mix into measuring cup; level with spatula. Makes about 7½ cups packed mix (enough for 5 single recipes of brownies).

To make brownies: Grease an 8x8x2-inch baking pan. In mixing bowl beat 2 *eggs* and 1 teaspoon *vanilla.* Add 1½ cups packed *Homemade Brownie Mix;* stir till nearly smooth. If desired, stir in ½ cup chopped *nuts,* semisweet *chocolate pieces, or butterscotch pieces.* Spread batter in prepared pan. Bake in 350° oven for 25 to 30 minutes or till done. Cool on wire rack. Cut into bars. Makes 16. (For 35 thinner brownies, double recipe. Bake in a greased 15x10x1-inch baking pan in 350° oven for 20 to 25 minutes.) Frost, if desired.

Peanut Butter Brownie Bars

1 cup peanut butter
½ cup sugar
1 egg
1½ cups packed Homemade Brownie Mix
2 eggs
1 teaspoon vanilla
¼ cup chopped peanuts

In mixer bowl combine peanut butter, sugar, and 1 egg; beat till well blended. Spread mixture in an ungreased 9x9x2-inch baking pan. Using 1½ cups packed Homemade Brownie Mix, 2 eggs, and the vanilla, prepare batter for a single recipe of brownies as directed in preceding recipe.

Spread batter evenly over peanut butter mixture in baking pan. Sprinkle with chopped peanuts. Bake in a 350° oven about 35 minutes or till done. Cool on wire rack. Cut into bars. Makes 20.

Granola Chip Cookies

1 package 3-dozen-size chocolate
   chip cookie mix
2 tablespoons honey
1 teaspoon finely shredded
   lemon peel
1 cup granola
½ cup shelled sunflower seed

Prepare cookie mix according to package directions; stir in honey and lemon peel. Stir in granola and sunflower seed. Drop from a teaspoon 2 inches apart onto an ungreased cookie sheet. Bake in 350° oven about 10 minutes or till done. Cool about 1 minute before removing to wire rack; cool thoroughly. Makes about 48.

Lemon Yogurt Drops

1 package 3-dozen-size sugar
   cookie mix
½ cup coconut
⅓ cup lemon yogurt
2 cups sifted powdered sugar
¼ cup lemon yogurt

Prepare cookie mix according to package directions. Stir in coconut and ⅓ cup yogurt. Drop from a teaspoon 2 inches apart onto an ungreased cookie sheet. Bake cookies according to package directions.

Cool about 1 minute before removing to wire rack. Cool thoroughly. In small mixing bowl beat powdered sugar and ¼ cup yogurt till smooth. Frost cookies. Makes about 36.

Peanut Butter and Jelly Sandwich Cookies

1 package 3-dozen-size peanut
   butter cookie mix
⅓ cup chopped peanuts
2 tablespoons honey
1 can creamy white frosting
   Grape *or* strawberry jelly

Prepare cookie mix according to package directions. Stir in peanuts and honey. Shape into 1-inch balls. Place 2 inches apart on an ungreased cookie sheet. With tines of a fork flatten in crisscross pattern. Bake in 375° oven about 8 minutes or till done. Cool about 1 minute before removing to wire rack; cool.

Frost the bottoms of *half* the cookies with some of the frosting. Spread about 1 teaspoon jelly on the bottom of each of the remaining cookies. Press together bottoms of a jelly cookie and a frosted cookie to form a sandwich. (Refrigerate any remaining frosting for another use.) Makes about 20.

Butterscotch Oatmeal Bars

1 package 3-dozen-size oatmeal
   cookie mix
2 tablespoons milk
1 6-ounce package (1 cup)
   butterscotch pieces
½ of a 7-ounce jar marshmallow
   creme

Grease an 8x8x2-inch baking pan. Prepare cookie mix according to package directions *except* stir in the milk with the other ingredients. Spread *half* of the oatmeal mixture into prepared pan. Sprinkle ¾ *cup* of the butterscotch pieces over oatmeal layer. Spread remaining oatmeal mixture over the layer of butterscotch pieces.

Bake in 350° oven for 30 to 35 minutes or till done. Cool 10 minutes on wire rack. Spread with marshmallow creme; sprinkle with the remaining butterscotch pieces. Return to oven; bake 10 minutes more. Cool on wire rack. Cut into bars. Makes 16.

Index

A-B

Almonds
  Almond Bars, 74
  Almond Cookies, 87
  Almond Filling, 27
  Almond Raspberry Torte, 27
  Sherry Almond Rounds, 80
Angel Cakes
  Angel Cake, 26
  Burnt Sugar-Pecan Angel
    Cake, 47
  Chocolate Angel Loaf, 26
  Chocolate-Flecked Angel
    Cake, 47
  Easy Angel Dessert, 26
  Spicy Angel Cake, 47
  Strawberry Angel Cake, 26
Apple Butter-Oatmeal Bars, 71
Apples
  Apple Upside-Down Cake, 46
  Dutch Apple Cake, 23
  Giant Peanut Butter-Apple
    Cookies, 59
Apricot Foldovers, 82
Bananas
  Banana Butter Frosting, 62
  Banana Drop Cookies, 62
  Banana Split Cake, 20
  Poppy Seed Cake, 17
Bar Cookies (see also *Brownies*)
  Almond Bars, 74
  Apple Butter-Oatmeal Bars, 71
  Butterscotch Oatmeal Bars, 92
  Cereal Peanut Bars, 71
  Cheesecake Cookies, 76
  Chocolate Chip Bars, 74
  Chocolate Revel Bars, 70
  Date Orange Bars, 76
  Double Chocolate Crumble
    Bars, 74
  Granola Raisin Bars, 91
  Lemon Squares, 75
  Mince Oatmeal Bars, 91
  Oatmeal Jam Bars, 71
  Old-Fashioned Raisin Bars, 75
  Peanut Butter Squares, 71
  Pecan Pie Bars, 75
  Pumpkin Bars, 76
  Raisin-Filled Granola Bars,
    75
  Seven-Layer Bars, 76
  Zucchini Bars, 76
Black Forest Cake, 11
Blonde Brownies, 74
Blueberry Lemon Cake, 42

Boston Cream Pie, 27
Bran Puff Cookies, 63
Brownies
  Blonde Brownies, 74
  Brownies, 91
  Chocolate Cream Cheese
    Brownies, 70
  Chocolate Syrup Brownies, 69
  Fudge Brownies, 69
  Homemade Brownie Mix, 91
  Peanut Butter Brownie Bars, 91
  Tri-Level Brownies, 70
Burnt Sugar Icing, 47
Burnt Sugar-Pecan Angel Cake, 47
Busy-Day Cake, 14
Butter Frosting, 50
Buttermilk White Cake, 16
Butterscotch Marble Cake, 44
Butterscotch Oatmeal Bars, 92
Buttery Cinnamon Cake, 23

C

Cake Mix Recipes
  Apple Upside-Down Cake, 46
  Blueberry Lemon Cake, 42
  Burnt Sugar-Pecan Angel Cake, 47
  Butterscotch Marble Cake, 44
  Cherry Devilicious Cake, 40
  Chocolate Date Cake, 40
  Chocolate-Flecked Angel Cake, 47
  Coconut Spice Cake Ring, 43
  Cream Cheese-Filled Cupcakes, 42
  Crunchy Apricot Cake, 43
  Date Nut Squares, 46
  Easy Pound Cake, 42
  Fudge Pudding Cake, 43
  Granola Ripple Cake, 44
  Holiday Fruitcake, 47
  Lemon Pound Cake, 44
  Orange Honey Cake, 42
  Peanut Butter-Topped Cake, 43
  Pineapple Pound Cake, 46
  Sherry Spice Cake, 46
  Spicy Angel Cake, 47
  Spicy Pumpkin Cake, 40
Cake Rolls
  Jelly Roll, 31
  Lincoln Log, 33
  Peppermint Ice Cream Roll, 33
  Pumpkin Cake Roll, 33
Candy Cane Cookies, 87
Candy Window Sugar Cookies, 78
Caramel Pecan Sauce, 53
Carrot Cake, 21
Cereal Peanut Bars, 71
Cheesecake Cookies, 76

Cherries
  Cherry Devilicious Cake, 40
  Cherry Filling, 11
  Cherry Sauce, 53
Chiffon Cakes
  Chocolate Chiffon Cake, 30
  Golden Chiffon Cake, 30
  Grapefruit Chiffon Cake, 30
  Maple-Nut Chiffon Cake, 28
  Marble Chiffon Cake, 30
  Tropical Chiffon Cake, 30
Chocolate (see also *Chocolate
    Chips*)
  Black Forest Cake, 11
  Cherry Devilicious Cake, 40
  Chocolate Angel Loaf, 26
  Chocolate Butter Frosting, 50
  Chocolate Chiffon Cake, 30
  Chocolate-Cinnamon Sheet
    Cake, 8
  Chocolate Coconut Slices, 66
  Chocolate Cream Cheese
    Brownies, 70
  Chocolate Crinkles, 84
  Chocolate Date Cake, 40
  Chocolate Drops, 90
  Chocolate-Flecked Angel Cake, 47
  Chocolate Glaze, 12
  Chocolate Icing, 52
  Chocolate Oatmeal Cake, 9
  Chocolate Revel Bars, 70
  Chocolate Sheet Cake, 8
  Chocolate Sour Cream
    Frosting, 51
  Chocolate Syrup Brownies, 69
  Chocolate Torte, 36
  Cocoa Drop Cookies, 60
  Cocoa Fudge Cake, 9
  Cream Cheese-Filled Cupcakes, 42
  Devil's Food Cake, 11
  Double Chocolate Crumble
    Bars, 74
  Double Chocolate Drops, 58
  Feathery Fudge Cake, 8
  Fudge Brownies, 69
  Fudge Frosting, 50
  Fudge Pudding Cake, 43
  German Chocolate Cake, 8
  Mocha Logs, 89
  Mocha Pound Cake, 35
  Nut Cake, 12
  Peanut Blossoms, 84
  Peanut Butter-Filled Fudge
    Cupcakes, 12
  Sour Cream Chocolate Cake, 12
  Tri-Level Brownies, 70
  Two-Tone Cookies, 59

Chocolate Chips
  Chocolate Chip Bars, 74
  Chocolate Chip Cake, 14
  Chocolate Chip Cookies, 57
  Chocolate Date Cake, 40
  Chocolate Drops, 90
  Double Chocolate Crumble
    Bars, 74
  Double Chocolate Drops, 58
  Granola Chip Cookies, 92
  Oatmeal Chippers, 58
  Seven-Layer Bars, 76
Cinnamon Blueberry Sauce, 53
Cinnamon Sheet Cake,
  Chocolate-, 8
Citrus Cake, Yellow, 16
Cocoa Drop Cookies, 60
Cocoa Fudge Cake, 9
Coconut
  Coconut Macaroons, 62
  Coconut Pecan Frosting, 51
  Coconut Spice Cake Ring, 43
  Coconut Sugar Cookies, 80
Cookie Mix Recipes
  Butterscotch Oatmeal Bars, 92
  Chocolate Drops, 90
  Granola Chip Cookies, 92
  Granola Raisin Bars, 91
  Homemade Brownie Mix, 91
  Homemade Cookie Mix, 90
  Lemon Yogurt Drops, 92
  Mince Oatmeal Bars, 91
  Oatmeal Raisin Cookies, 90
  Orange Coconut Drops, 90
  Peanut Butter and Jelly
    Sandwich Cookies, 92
  Peanut Butter Brownie Bars, 91
  Peanut Molasses Cookies, 90
Cranberry Nut Fruitcake, 39
Cranberry-Pear Upside-Down
  Cake, 17
Cream Cheese
  Cheesecake Cookies, 76
  Cream Cheese-Filled
    Cupcakes, 42
  Cream Cheese Frosting, 51
  Cream Cheese Icing, 52
  Peanut Butter-Filled Fudge
    Cupcakes, 12
Crunchy Apricot Cake, 43
Cupcakes, Cream Cheese-
  Filled, 42
Cupcakes, Peanut Butter-Filled
  Fudge, 12
Currant Pound Cake, 35
Cutout Cookies
  Apricot Foldovers, 82
  Candy Window Sugar Cookies, 78
  Coconut Sugar Cookies, 80

Cutout Cookies *(continued)*
  Gingerbread Cutouts, 79
  Jam-Filled Cookies, 80
  Lebkuchen, 82
  Peanut Butter Cutouts, 79
  Rolled Spice Cookies, 79
  Rolled Sugar Cookies, 78
  Scotch Shortbread, 79
  Sherry Almond Rounds, 80
  Sour Cream Sugar Cookies, 78
  Springerle, 82
  Viennese Butter Rounds, 80

D-F

Dark Fruitcake, 39
Dates
  Date Cake, 20
  Date Filling, 52
  Date Nut Squares, 46
  Date Orange Bars, 76
  Date Pinwheels, 68
Devil's Food Cake, 11
Double Chocolate Crumble
  Bars, 74
Double Chocolate Drops, 58
Double Peanut Butter Cookies, 66
Double Peanut Cookies, 84
Drop Cookies
  Banana Drop Cookies, 62
  Bran Puff Cookies, 63
  Chocolate Chip Cookies, 57
  Chocolate Drops, 90
  Cocoa Drop Cookies, 60
  Coconut Macaroons, 62
  Double Chocolate Drops, 58
  Giant Peanut Butter-Apple
    Cookies, 59
  Ginger Creams, 64
  Granola Chip Cookies, 92
  Hermits, 63
  Jam-Topped Drop Cookies, 60
  Lacy Oatmeal Crisps, 59
  Lemon Tea Cookies, 60
  Lemon Yogurt Drops, 92
  Mincemeat Cookies, 63
  No-Bake Drop Cookies, 59
  Oatmeal Chippers, 58
  Oatmeal Raisin Cookies, 90
  Orange Coconut Drops, 90
  Orange Drop Cookies, 62
  Peanut Molasses Cookies, 90
  Pecan Crispies, 60
  Pumpkin Drop Cookies, 62
  Ranger Cookies, 63
  Toffee Drop Cookies, 64
  Two-Tone Cookies, 59
  Wheat Germ-Molasses Date
    Cookies, 64

Dutch Apple Cake, 23
Easy Angel Dessert, 26
Easy Pound Cake, 42
Feathery Fudge Cake, 8
Fig Filling, 52
Fillings
  Almond Filling, 27
  Cherry Filling, 11
  Date Filling, 52
  Fig Filling, 52
  Lemon Filling, 53
  Pineapple Filling, 89
  Vanilla Cream Filling, 52
Fluffy White Frosting, 50
Frostings
  Banana Butter Frosting, 62
  Burnt Sugar Icing, 47
  Butter Frosting, 50
  Chocolate Butter Frosting, 50
  Chocolate Glaze, 12
  Chocolate Icing, 52
  Chocolate Sour Cream
    Frosting, 51
  Coconut Pecan Frosting, 51
  Cream Cheese Frosting, 51
  Cream Cheese Icing, 52
  Fluffy White Frosting, 50
  Fudge Frosting, 50
  Golden Butter Frosting, 11
  Lemon Butter Frosting, 50
  Lemon Glaze, 82
  Lemon Icing, 87
  Mocha Butter Frosting, 58
  Mocha Frosting, 51
  Orange Butter Frosting, 50
  Peanut Butter Frosting, 50
  Penuche Frosting, 52
  Peppermint-Stick Frosting, 51
  Powdered Sugar Icing, 52
  Seafoam Frosting, 51
  Seven-Minute Frosting, 51
  Shadow Icing, 54
Fruitcakes
  Cranberry Nut Fruitcake, 39
  Dark Fruitcake, 39
  Holiday Fruitcake, 47
  Last-Minute Fruitcake, 39
  Light Fruitcake, 38
Fudge Brownies, 69
Fudge Frosting, 50
Fudge Pudding Cake, 43

G-N

German Chocolate Cake, 8
Giant Peanut Butter-Apple
  Cookies, 59
Gingerbread, 21
Gingerbread Cutouts, 79

Ginger Creams, 64
Ginger Crinkles, 83
Golden Butter Frosting, 11
Golden Chiffon Cake, 30
Granola
    Granola Chip Cookies, 92
    Granola Raisin Bars, 91
    Granola Ripple Cake, 44
    Raisin-Filled Granola Bars, 75
Grapefruit Chiffon Cake, 30
Hermits, 63
Holiday Fruitcake, 47
Homemade Brownie Mix, 91
Homemade Cookie Mix, 90
Honey Cake, Milk and, 16
Honey Cake, Orange, 42
Individual Fluted Tube
    Cakes, 13
Jam
    Jam-Filled Cookies, 80
    Jam Thumbprints, 87
    Jam-Topped Drop Cookies, 60
Jelly Roll, 31
Kringla, 86
Lacy Oatmeal Crisps, 59
Lady Baltimore Cake, 14
Last-Minute Fruitcake, 39
Lebkuchen, 82
Lemons
    Blueberry Lemon Cake, 42
    Lemon Butter Frosting, 50
    Lemon Filling, 53
    Lemon Glaze, 82
    Lemon Icing, 87
    Lemon Pound Cake, 44
    Lemon Rounds, 87
    Lemon Squares, 75
    Lemon Tea Cookies, 60
    Lemon Yogurt Drops, 92
Light Fruitcake, 38
Lincoln Log, 33
Maple-Nut Chiffon Cake, 28
Marble Chiffon Cake, 30
Marble Pound Cake, 36
Milk and Honey Cake, 16
Mincemeat Cookies, 63
Mince Oatmeal Bars, 91
Mocha
    Mocha Butter Frosting, 58
    Mocha Frosting, 51
    Mocha Logs, 89
    Mocha Pound Cake, 35
Molasses
    Ginger Creams, 64
    Oatmeal Molasses Cookies, 86
    Peanut Molasses Cookies, 90
    Pumpkin Molasses Cake, 21
    Wheat Germ-Molasses Date
        Cookies, 64

No-Bake Cookies
    Cereal Peanut Bars, 71
    No-Bake Drop Cookies, 59
Nut Cake, 12
Nutmeg Cake, 20

O-Q

Oatmeal
    Apple Butter-Oatmeal Bars, 71
    Butterscotch Oatmeal Bars, 92
    Chocolate Oatmeal Cake, 9
    Lacy Oatmeal Crisps, 59
    Mince Oatmeal Bars, 91
    No-Bake Drop Cookies, 59
    Oatmeal Chippers, 58
    Oatmeal Cookies, 84
    Oatmeal Jam Bars, 71
    Oatmeal Molasses Cookies, 86
    Oatmeal Raisin Cookies, 90
    Oatmeal Refrigerator Cookies, 66
Old-Fashioned Raisin Bars, 75
Oranges
    Date Orange Bars, 76
    Orange Butter Frosting, 50
    Orange Coconut Drops, 90
    Orange Drop Cookies, 62
    Orange Honey Cake, 42
    Orange Refrigerator Cookies, 68
Peanut Blossoms, 84
Peanut Butter
    Double Peanut Butter
        Cookies, 66
    Double Peanut Cookies, 84
    Giant Peanut Butter-Apple
        Cookies, 59
    Peanut Blossoms, 84
    Peanut Butter and Jelly Cake, 17
    Peanut Butter and Jelly
        Sandwich Cookies, 92
    Peanut Butter Brownie Bars, 91
    Peanut Butter Cookies, 84
    Peanut Butter Cutouts, 79
    Peanut Butter-Filled Fudge
        Cupcakes, 12
    Peanut Butter Frosting, 50
    Peanut Butter Squares, 71
    Peanut Butter-Topped Cake, 43
Peanuts
    Double Peanut Cookies, 84
    Oatmeal Chippers, 58
    Peanut Molasses Cookies, 90
Pecans
    Pecan Crispies, 60
    Pecan Pie Bars, 75
    Pecan Tassies, 89
    Sugar Pecan Crisps, 66
Penuche Frosting, 52
Peppermint Ice Cream Roll, 33

Peppermint-Stick Frosting, 51
Petits Fours, 14
Pineapple
    Pineapple-Filled Spritz, 89
    Pineapple Filling, 89
    Pineapple Pound Cake, 46
    Pineapple Upside-Down Cake, 17
Poppy Seed Cake, 17
Pound Cakes
    Chocolate Torte, 36
    Currant Pound Cake, 35
    Easy Pound Cake, 42
    Lemon Pound Cake, 44
    Marble Pound Cake, 36
    Mocha Pound Cake, 35
    Pineapple Pound Cake, 46
    Pound Cake, 35
    Sour Cream Pound Cake, 36
Powdered Sugar Icing, 52
Pressed Cookies
    Mocha Logs, 89
    Pineapple-Filled Spritz, 89
    Spritz, 89
Pumpkin
    Pumpkin Bars, 76
    Pumpkin Cake Roll, 33
    Pumpkin Drop Cookies, 62
    Pumpkin Molasses Cake, 21
    Spicy Pumpkin Cake, 40

R-S

Raisins
    Bran Puff Cookies, 63
    Granola Raisin Bars, 91
    Hermits, 63
    Oatmeal Raisin Cookies, 90
    Old-Fashioned Raisin
        Bars, 75
    Poppy Seed Cake, 17
    Pumpkin Drop Cookies, 62
    Raisin-Filled Granola
        Bars, 75
Ranger Cookies, 63
Refrigerator Cookies, 65
Rolled Spice Cookies, 79
Rolled Sugar Cookies, 78
Sandies, 83
Santa's Whiskers, 68
Sauces
    Caramel Pecan Sauce, 53
    Cherry Sauce, 53
    Cinnamon Blueberry Sauce, 53
    Strawberry Sauce, 53
Scotch Shortbread, 79
Seafoam Frosting, 51
Seven-Layer Bars, 76
Seven-Minute Frosting, 51
Shadow Icing, 54

Shaped Cookies (see also
  Pressed Cookies)
  Almond Cookies, 87
  Candy Cane Cookies, 87
  Chocolate Crinkles, 84
  Double Peanut Cookies, 84
  Ginger Crinkles, 83
  Jam Thumbprints, 87
  Kringla, 86
  Lemon Rounds, 87
  Oatmeal Cookies, 84
  Oatmeal Molasses Cookies, 86
  Peanut Blossoms, 84
  Peanut Butter and Jelly
    Sandwich Cookies, 92
  Peanut Butter Cookies, 84
  Pecan Tassies, 89
  Sandies, 83
  Shaped Sugar Cookies, 86
  Snickerdoodles, 86
Sherry Almond Rounds, 80
Sherry Spice Cake, 46
Silver White Layer Cake, 16
Sliced Cookies
  Chocolate Coconut Slices, 66
  Date Pinwheels, 68
  Double Peanut Butter Cookies, 66
  Oatmeal Refrigerator Cookies, 66
  Orange Refrigerator Cookies, 68
  Refrigerator Cookies, 65
  Santa's Whiskers, 68
  Sugar Pecan Crisps, 66
  Whole Wheat Refrigerator
    Cookies, 65
Snickerdoodles, 86
Sour Cream
  Banana Split Cake, 20
  Sour Cream Chocolate Cake, 12
  Sour Cream Pound Cake, 36
  Sour Cream Sugar Cookies, 78
Spice Cakes
  Buttery Cinnamon Cake, 23
  Carrot Cake, 21
  Cherry Devilicious Cake, 40
  Chocolate-Cinnamon Sheet
    Cake, 8
  Coconut Spice Cake Ring, 43
  Dutch Apple Cake, 23
  Gingerbread 21
  Nut Cake, 12
  Nutmeg Cake, 20
  Pumpkin Molasses Cake, 21
  Sherry Spice Cake, 46
  Spicy Angel Cake, 47
  Spicy Pumpkin Cake, 40
Sponge Cakes
  Almond Raspberry Torte, 27
  Boston Cream Pie, 27
  Sponge Cake, 27

Springerle, 82
Spritz, 89
Strawberry Angel Cake, 26
Strawberry Sauce, 53
Sugar Cookies
  Candy Window Sugar
    Cookies, 78
  Coconut Sugar Cookies, 80
  Rolled Sugar Cookies, 78
  Shaped Sugar Cookies, 86
  Sour Cream Sugar Cookies,
    78
  Sugar Pecan Crisps, 66

T-Z

Toffee Drop Cookies, 64
Tortes
  Almond Raspberry Torte, 27
  Black Forest Cake, 11
  Chocolate Torte, 36
Tri-Level Brownies, 70
Tropical Chiffon Cake, 30
Two-Tone Cookies, 59
Vanilla Cream Filling, 52
Viennese Butter Rounds, 80
Wheat Germ-Molasses Date
  Cookies, 64
White Cakes
  Buttermilk White Cake, 16
  Chocolate Chip Cake, 14
  Lady Baltimore Cake, 14
  Petits Fours, 14
  Silver White Layer Cake, 16
  White Cake Supreme, 14
Whole Wheat Cookies, 65
Yellow Cakes
  Banana Split Cake, 20
  Blueberry Lemon Cake, 42
  Busy-Day Cake, 14
  Cranberry-Pear Upside-Down
    Cake, 17
  Crunchy Apricot Cake, 43
  Date Cake, 20
  Individual Fluted Tube
    Cakes, 13
  Milk and Honey Cake, 16
  Orange Honey Cake, 42
  Peanut Butter and Jelly
    Cake, 17
  Peanut Butter-Topped
    Cake, 43
  Pineapple Upside-Down
    Cake, 17
  Poppy Seed Cake, 17
  Yellow Cake, 13
  Yellow Citrus Cake, 16
Yogurt Drops, Lemon, 92
Zucchini Bars, 76

Tips and Techniques

Angel and Sponge Cake
  Techniques, 25
Baking Pan Variations, 9
Bar Cookie Techniques, 69
Cake Making Tips, 21
Cake Roll Techniques, 31
Chiffon Cake Techniques, 28
Chocolate Cake Techniques, 7
Cutout Cookie Techniques, 78
Decorating Cakes and
  Cookies, 54-55
Drop Cookie Techniques, 57
Easy Slicing Tip, 68
Frosting a Cake, 49
Fruitcake Techniques, 38
High Altitude Baking Chart, 23
Making Sour Milk, 16
Pound Cake Techniques, 35
Shaped Cookie Techniques, 83
Sliced Cookie Techniques, 65
Storing and Freezing
  Cookies, 58
White, Yellow, and Spice Cake
  Techniques, 13